THE AMISH RECIPE PROJECT

By Kevin Williams

The Amish Recipe Project is a unique collection of recipes from plain people across the United States and Canada. Food traditions are fading, tastes and recipes are becoming homogenized as recipes morph into a bland sameness across cultures in the United States. This book is an attempt to capture and catalogue plain culinary traditions before they disappear.

During the course of writing our hardcover cookbook, *Amish Cooks Across America* (**Andrews McMeel Publishing, scheduled for release in fall 2012),** we collected hundreds of recipes. Only about 100 recipes could make the cut for *Amish Cooks Across America*, but the rest were too good sounding just to let languish in a box in my office. So we are publishing them in book form for you to enjoy.

Many of these recipes are "cast offs"….they just didn't fit the mission of *Amish Cooks Across America*. Recipes like "Broccoli Ramen Salad" didn't fit the mold of traditional Amish cooking so we didn't use it in ACAA, but it still is an interesting recipe to share. And some recipes were just plain mystifying: Skier's French Toast?

Whereas ACAA is a collection of recipes from primarily Amish Cooks, recipes in this book come from plain communities of all stripes. There are raisin cookies from a German Baptist settlement and red beet jelly from the most conservative Schwartzentruber Amish. So this book represents a wonderful mix of culinary surprises from across the plain spectrum.

These recipes are also being published "as is" and it's not pure laziness that is motivating this format, but also a desire for readers to experience the recipes as I do. Part of the charm of the recipes is how I receive them with folksy instructions like "bake until done" or "add enough sugar until sweet." So this book should not be looked at as an exercise in frustration but rather a "treasure hunt" for truly authentic Amish recipes.

But as noted earlier, this is more than just a book, it is an interactive project meant to catalogue and preserve. So we are inviting and requesting readers to try recipes, edit them, sample them and then share their experiences at amishcookonline.com   If you aren't internet saavy, that's okay…share your experiences by writing:

The Amish Recipe Project
PO BOX 157
Middletown, Ohio 45042

But if you are internet-wise we'd love you to share your experiences with these recipes and see photos of your process and final product. Photos can be uploaded by going to www.amishcookonline and clicking on the "Amish Recipe Project" tile. In working together we can all be a part of what is a worthy project: cataloguing and preserving traditional Amish cooking and culture.

Many times fans of the Amish Cook will request a book of "just recipes", so hopefully this book fulfills your wish. The recipes are a motley collection of desserts, entrees, vegetables, and appetizers in no particular order. The book is a reflection of the changes occurring in Amish cooking which for most of its American existence consisted generally of classic farm fare. As the Amish have become less insular of a people their food come to reflect that.

Items like homemade "breakfast burritos" have become staples on the menus of most Amish cooks. Instant puddings, cans of soup, and saltines are now just as common in Amish kitchens as lard and freshly made bread.

I'd like to thank the many Amish, Mennonite, and other plain cooks who contributed, among them: Dorcas Raber, Mrs. Noah Gingerich, Katie Lehman, John Mast, Freda Yoder, Misheal Kopp, Edna Fehr, Malinda Beachy, and Jake Schwartz.

We hope you enjoy this journey.

Ground Beef 5 Shepherd's Pie	Soups
12 Sloppy Joes	7 chili
16 Taco Salad	8 cheesy veg.
17 Curly Fry Casserole	34 Borscht beef-veg
25 Country Casserole	36 Bean soup
27 Mushroom burgers	37 chili
30 Beef Pot Pie	47 Potato soup
38 Cheddar Meatloaf	49 chicken, corn, rivel
40 Meat Pie	50 rivels
44 Meatballs	52 Cold Day Soup
45 Sweet Sour meatballs	53 Corn chowder
46 Mennonite meatballs	54 Garden Veg.
55 Meatloaf	
56 Ground Beef - Noodles	
57 Layered dinner	

MAIN DISHES

Chicken	Ham - Sausage
13 Roast chicken	5 BBQ ham
18 Chicken Casserole	6. sausage
23 " "	14 Ham casserole
24 oven fried chicken	26 sausage casserole
31 chicken loaf	28 Ham loaf
39 chicken + gravy	41 Ham potato Cass
43 chicken Pot Pie	42 Baked noodles + ham
50 chicken dressing Cass.	9, 10 French toast
	13 . omelet
7. Deep Dish Taco squares	19, 20, 21, 22, 31
11. Pizza	Pancakes
48 Liver BBQ	
59, Plain dumpling	
32	

SHEPHERD'S PIE

1 pound ground beef
4 cups mashed potatoes
4 ounces cream cheese
1 cup shredded Cheddar cheese
4 cups mixed vegetables (from garden or frozen)
1 cup beef gravy

Brown meat in skillet. Drain. Mix mashed potatoes, cream cheese, and 1/2 cup of shredded cheddar cheese. Stir vegetables and gravy into meat and spoon into 9-inch baking dish. Cover with potato mixture. Sprinkle remaining shredded cheese over top. Bake at 375 for 20 minutes or until heated well. Parsley flakes and paprika can be sprinkled over cheese.

BARBECUED HAM

3 tablespoons butter
1/2 cup onion
1 cup ketchup
2 tablespoons brown sugar
2 teaspoons mustard
1/4 cup vinegar
1/2 cup water

1 1/2 pound chopped ham
Clear-jel

Cook together and add clear-jel to thicken slightly. Enjoy!

FAVORITE SAUSAGE SEASONING

Editor's note: this recipe, typical of many submitted, contained simply a list of ingredients and one line of instruction. This might be frustrating to a non-Amish cook, but an experienced Amish Cook probably wouldn't even use a recipe!

25 pounds sausage
3/4 cup salt
5 tablespoons black pepper
5 tablespoon sage
2 tablespoons garlic powder
2 teaspoons nutmeg
2 teaspoons paprika
1 teaspoon red pepper
1/3 cup liquid smoke

We like to put seasoning on the meat before grinding.

HOMEMADE CHILI SOUP

Editor's Note: This recipe format is very typical, was just submitted as a cluster of sentences on an index card.

Melt 1 tablespoon butter in a frying pan. Add 2 onions, chopped fine and fry until brown. Add 1 pound hamburger and cook until all is well done. Transfer to a kettle and add 1 pint strained kidney beans, 1 pint tomato juice, 1 teaspoon chili powder, and 1 quart water. Salt to taste. Serve hot.

DEEP DISH TACO SQUARES

Editor's Note: This has become a popular recipe in Amish communities, but the instructions are a little spare.

1 1/2 pound hamburger
1/2 cup sour cream
1/3 cup mayonnaise
1 tablespoon chopped onion
1 cup Bisquick
1/4 cup cold water
1/2 cup shredded cheese
Taco seasoning or pizza sauce

Heat oven to 375. Brown hamburger and drain. Mix sour cream, mayo, cheese, and onion. Set aside. Mix Bisquick and water until soft dough forms. Put in pan pressing dough up sides. Layer beef on dough. Spoon sour cream mixture on top. Bake 25 - 30 minutes. Double batch makes 9 X 13 cake pan.

CHEESY VEGETABLE SOUP

2 1/2 cups potatoes, diced

1 onion, diced

8 ounces of frozen mixed vegetables

1 diced green pepper

1 tablespoon chicken base

2 cans cream of celery soup

2 cups velveeta cheese

Cook vegetables until tender. Add soup and cheese. Don't boil.

NUTTY BAKED FRENCH TOAST

1 loaf of bread, sliced

8 eggs

2 cups milk

2 cups half and half

2 teaspoons vanilla

1/2 teaspoons nutmeg

1/2 teaspoons cinnamon

3/4 cup butter

1 1/2 cup brown sugar

3 tablespoons dark corn syrup

1 1/3 cup chopped nuts

Generously grease 9 X 13 inch pan. Fill pan with bread slices to within 1/2" of top. Blend together eggs, milk, half and half, vanilla, and spices. Pour over bread. Cover and refrigerate overnight. Combine topping ingredients and set aside until time to bake toast. Heat topping till butter is melted. Spread over bread. Bake at 350 for 50 minutes till puffed and golden. If it browns too quickly, put foil on top. 10–12 servings.

SKIER'S FRENCH TOAST

Editor's Note: title of this recipe is puzzling. Anyone have any ideas of how it got its name?

2 tablespoons Karo

1/2 cup oleo

1 cup brown sugar

12 to 16 slices of bread

5 eggs

1 1/2 cups milk

Vanilla

Salt

Mix first 3 ingredients together in a saucepan. Bring to a boil then pour into bottom of a 9 X 13 inch pan. Place slices of bread over syrup. Beat together eggs, milk, vanilla, and salt. Pour over bread and refrigerate overnight. Sprinkle cinnamon on top of bread then the next morning bake at 350 for 45 minutes. Cut into squares and invert.

TOP-NOTCH PIZZA

A young girl from Michigan stayed in our community of Flat Rock, Illinois for a year. She and her sister came up with this recipe. - Dorcas Raber - Flat Rock, Illinois

Bake your favorite pizza crust in a 13 X 18" greased pan. Add your favorite seasonings.

Top with the following:

Velveeta cheese slices

1 - 1 1/2 cups sour cream mixed with some Hidden Valley Ranch Dip Mix.

Grilled turkey breasts with spices of your choice

Ham chunks

Pepperoni slices

Diced peppers

Diced onions

Barbecue sauce to put on top:

1/2 cup ketchup

1 teaspoon Worcestershire sauce

1/4 teaspoon liquid smoke

3 tablespoons brown sugar

1/2 teaspoon chili powder

1/4 teaspoon garlic salt

1/4 teaspoon onion salt

1/2 teaspoon mustard

Top with shredded cheese. Bake at 350.

SLOPPY JOES

2 pounds ground beef

1 1/4 cup ketchup

1 tablespoon brown sugar

1/2 teaspoon salt

1/2 teaspoon chili powder

8 hamburger buns

Cook beef and onions till no longer pink. Add rest of ingredients and simmer 35- 40 minutes.

OMELET CASSEROLE

1 stick melted butter in a 9 X 13 inch pan. Beat 20 eggs, 2 cups milk, 1/4 teaspoon pepper and 1/2 teaspoon salt until blended. Stir in 1 1/2 cups Swiss cheese and 1 1/2 cups ham. Pour into dish. Bake uncovered at 350 for 40–45 minutes or until knife inserted in center comes out clean.

ROAST CHICKEN

Editor's Note: A simple recipe submitted from the relatively new Amish settlement of Vanceburg, Kentucky

1 broiler, cut into pieces
1 stick oleo, melted
1/2 cup vinegar
Lawry's seasoning salt

Put chicken pieces into a 9 X 13 pan and cover with vinegar and oleo. Sprinkle with Lawry's. Bake at 350 to 400 for 1 1/2 hour. Do not turn while it is in over. A very easy way to have good chicken!

HOMEMADE SANDWICH SPREAD

6 onions

6 peppers

6 green tomatoes

6 cucumbers

6 carrots

Grind. Put in salt overnight. Drain. Boil 25 minutes in 1 pint vinegar, 4 cups sugar. Add 3/4 cup flour to 1 cup prepared mustard. Boil 10 minutes longer. Yield: 8 pints.

UNDERGROUND HAM CASSEROLE

Editor's note: Interesting title, anyone have any ideas as to where this got its name?

4 cups chunked ham

4 tablespoons margarine

1/2 cup chopped onion

1 tablespoons Worcestershire sauce

2 cans cream of mushroom soup

1 cup milk
2 cups cubed Velveeta cheese
4 quarts mashed potatoes
16 ounces of sour cream
Browned crumbled bacon

Combine ham, margarine, onions, and Worcestershire sauce. Cook until onions are tender. Place in bottom of a medium sized roasting pan. In a saucepan heat together soup, milk, and cheese until cheese is melted. Place over top of ham mixture. Mash cooked potatoes, using no salt or milk, and mix with sour cream. Spread over the top of mixture and sprinkle with bacon. Bake at 350 for 20 minutes or until hot. This is a very tasty casserole.

Variation: instead of the ham, use precooked cubed chicken breast. And also precooked (not too soft) broccoli and cauliflower. Delicious!

TACO SALAD

1 pound ground beef, fried

1 - 2 heads iceburg lettuce, chopped

3 medium tomatoes, diced

1 pint kidney beans, cooked, rinsed and drained

1/2 cup chopped celery

1/2 cup chopped green peppers

1 cup cubed cheddar cheese

Taco chips

Dressing:

1/2 cup vegetable oil

1/4 cup vinegar

1/2 cup catsup

Mix all ingredients in a large bowl until well-blended. Pour dressing over all just before serving. Serves 12.

CURLY FRY TORTILLA CASSEROLE

Editor's Note: This may be one of the most unusual recipes we received during the course of collecting recipes for this book!

2 pounds hamburger

1/3 onion, chopped

1 can cream of mushroom soup

1 can cream of chicken soup

8 ounces sour cream

10 tortillas (flour) cut into 1" squares

2/3 cup salsa or pizza sauce

1 1/3 cup shredded cheese

Velveeta cheese

16 ounces of curly fries

Seasoned salt

Brown hamburger and onions. Mix in soups, sour cream, tortillas, salsa, and shredded cheese. Put into a roaster. Bake at 325 to 350 until heated thoroughly. Remove from oven. Top with melted velveeta and curly fries (made according to directions on package). Sprinkle with seasoned salt.

CHICKEN CASSEROLE

1 quart carrots, diced

4 quarts potatoes, diced

1 pint celery, diced

1 large onion

2 quarts frozen peas

4 to 5 quarts chicken

Miller's soup base, 3 tablespoons plus 2 1/4 quarter water for stock

Cook vegetables and deboned chicken in cooker for 1 hour and 30 minutes.

AMISH APPLE PANCAKES

2 Granny Smith apples, peeled, cored, and sliced

1 c. flour

1 c. milk

6 eggs

1 tsp. vanilla

1/4 tsp. salt

1/4 tsp. nutmeg

2 tbsp. butter

In mixer or blender, beat flour, milk, eggs, vanilla, salt, and nutmeg; set aside. Heat oven to 475 degrees. In cast iron skillet for 5 minutes, add 2 tablespoons butter; melt. Add sliced apples and fry 2 to 3 minutes. Pour mixture over apples. Bake at 475 degrees for 15 minutes. Reduce heat to 425 degrees for 8 to 10 minutes. Sprinkle with powdered sugar. Cut in wedges. Serve with syrup or jam and bacon.

TASTY PANCAKES

2 beaten eggs

2 cups sour milk

1 teaspoon baking soda

2 1/4 cups flour

2 teaspoons baking powder

1 teaspoon salt

4 tablespoons melted butter

2 teaspoons sugar

If sweet milk is used, mmit soda and increase the baking powder to 3 teaspoons. Beat egg until light. Add milk. Sift flour with baking powder, salt, and sugar. Beat flour mixture into egg and milk mixture. Add melted butter. Beat until smooth. Make in hot iron pan. Serve with hot maple syrup and sausage.

AMISH WAFFLES

2/3 c. all purpose flour

2/3 c. sifted cake flour

1 c. milk

1 3/4 tsp. baking powder

1 1/3 whole eggs, well beaten

3 1/2 tbsp. butter or margarine

3/4 tsp. vanilla extract

TOPPING

1 c. water

7 tbsp. sugar

1 1/4 tsp. white corn syrup

2 Pinches red food coloring

4 tsp. cornstarch

2/3 whole (3 oz.) raspberry flavored gelatin

5 1/4 sol. oz. frozen blueberries, defrosted

5 1/4 sol. oz. frozen raspberries, defrosted

Vanilla ice cream, optional

Mix batter ingredients together in order just until smooth. Bake in waffle iron according to manufacturer's directions. For topping, combine water, sugar, corn syrup, food coloring and cornstarch in saucepan; cook over medium heat until thickened. Remove from heat; add gelatin, stirring until dissolved. Cook, add berries. Serve warm over waffles with a scoop of vanilla ice cream, if desired. Yield: 4 servings.

AMISH PANCAKES

2 c. cake flour

2 tsp. baking powder

1 tsp. salt

1/2 c. sugar1 egg

1 c. milk

1/4 c. shortening, melted

Measure sifted flour into sifter, add baking powder, salt and sugar. Beat eggs in bowl. Add milk and blend. Sift dry ingredients into mixture gradually. Add melted shortening. Beat with mixer. Bake on hot griddle.

AMISH CHICKEN CASSEROLE

8 oz. noodles, cooked

2 c. cooked chicken, cubed

2 c. chicken broth (can used canned)

1 c. milk

1 can mushrooms

2 tsp. salt

1/2 tsp. pepper

1/2 c. margarine

1/3 c. flour

1/3 c. grated Parmesan cheese

Melt margarine, then add flour and stir until smooth. Gradually add milk and broth, then seasonings and mushrooms. Combine chicken, cooked noodles, and prepared sauce. Put in ungreased 9 inch x 13 inch x 2 inch baking pan and top with Parmesan cheese.

AMISH OVEN FRIED CHICKEN

1/3 c. vegetable oil

1/3 c. butter

1 c. all-purpose flour

1 tsp. salt

2 tsp. black pepper

2 tsp. paprika

1 tsp. garlic salt

1 tsp. dried marjoram

8 or 9 pieces chicken

Place oil and butter in a shallow cooking pan and place in 375 degree oven to melt butter, set aside. In a large paper sack combine dry ingredients. Roll the chicken pieces 3 at a time in butter and oil then drop into a sack and shake to cover. Place on a plate until all pieces are coated. Leave any excess butter and oil in pan. Place chicken in the pan skin side down or its just as good if you remove all the skin first. Bake at 375 degrees for 45 minutes with spatula, turn chicken pieces over and bake 5 to 10 minutes longer or until crust begins to bubble.

AMISH COUNTRY CASSEROLE

1 lb. beef chunks or ground beef

1 chopped onion

1 can tomato soup

1 lb. egg noodles

1 can cream of mushroom soup

1 tbsp. olive oil

Saute chopped onion in olive oil. Add beef. Cook well. Add can of tomato soup undiluted. Cook egg noodles according to directions on package. Drain well. Add can of cream of mushroom soup, undiluted. Grease casserole dish. Place 1/2 of beef mixture in bottom of casserole. Add 1/2 of noodle mixture. Put rest of beef on noodles. Add remaining noodles. If desired, sprinkle paprika lightly over top of noodles. Bake in 375 degree oven for 20–25 minutes, or until bubbly.

SAUSAGE COTTAGE CHEESE CASSEROLE

1 pound pork sausage

1 onion; chopped

1 Bell pepper; chopped

6 - 12 eggs; lightly beaten

4 cups frozen shredded hash browns; thawed

2 cups Cheddar cheese; shredded

1 1/2 cups small curd cottage cheese

1 1/4 cups Swiss Cheese; shredded

In a large frying pan, brown sausage with onion and pepper, stirring to crumble sausage. Drain. In a large bowl, mix all remaining ingredients (except salsa), and stir in sausage mixture. Transfer to a greased 13x9" baking dish. May sprinkle extra cheddar cheese on top. Bake at 350 for 35-40 minutes. Delicious served with a spoonful of salsa.

AMISH MUSHROOM BURGERS

1 1/4 lb ground beef

1 teaspoon salt, divided

1/4 teaspoon plus 1/8 teaspoon black pepper, divided

1 tablespoon olive oil

1/2 cup thinly sliced yellow onion

4 ounces sliced exotic mushrooms or 2 cups sliced button mushrooms

2 teaspoons Worcestershire sauce

4 slices Colby Jack cheese

4 onion rolls, split, lightly toasted or grilled

Combine the beef, 3/4 teaspoon salt and 1/4 teaspoon black pepper. Shape into 4 patties, 1/2-inch thick.

Grill the patties, 4 to 5 minutes per side or until the internal temperature reaches 160°F.

Meanwhile, heat the olive oil in a large nonstick skillet over medium-high heat. Add the onions and cook for 2 minutes. Stir in the mushrooms, Worcestershire sauce, remaining 1/4 teaspoon salt and 1/8 teaspoon black pepper. Cook and stir for 5 minutes or until tender.

Place cheese slices over patties during the last minute of cooking. Serve mushroom burgers in rolls topped with mushroom and onion mixture.

YUMMY HAM LOAF

2 lb. Ham Loaf

1 cup bread crumbs

2 eggs

3/4 to 1 cup milk

salt and pepper to taste

Mix all ingredients. Shape in loaf and place in a roasting pan. Bake at 350 for about 1 1/2 hrs. After 1/2 hour pour the following sauce over the loaf:

3/4 cup brown sugar

1 tsp. dry mustard

1/2 cup water

1/2 cup vinegar

Mix and bring to a boil before pouring over ham loaf. Serves 8.

MENNONITE BROWN FLOUR SOUP

6 medium potatoes

3 C. water

3 C. milk

3 T. flour

3 T. butter

Salt, pepper and parsley

Peel and cut potatoes in slices. Boil them in salted water until tender. Add the milk and let simmer. Meanwhile brown the flour in the melted butter, stirring all the time over low heat; add it to the soup, stirring until the mixture thickens. Sprinkle with parsley and pepper. Serve with buttered crumbs, or squares of fried bread, or pretzels on top. You might boil some sliced onion with the potatoes, if you like.

OLD-FASHIONED BEEF POT PIE

2 pounds stewing beef

6 cups water

1 1/2 teaspoons salt

6 medium size potatoes

2 cups all-purpose flour

1 egg

3 tablespoons milk or water

1 teaspoon minced onion

1 teaspoon minced parsley

Cook meat in salt water until it is tender.

Remove meat from broth; add minced onion and parsley to broth. Bring to the boiling point and add alternate layers of cubed potatoes and squares of dough.

Add meat and stir through pot pie.

To make dough, beat egg and add milk. Add flour to make a stiff dough. Roll out paper thin and cut into 1-inch squares. Keep broth boiling while adding dough squares in order to keep them from packing together. Cover and cook for 20 minutes, adding more water if needed.

CHICKEN LOAF

2 c. cooked chicken
1 c. soft bread crumbs
2 tbsp. parsley
2 tbsp. celery
1 tsp. salt
2 eggs
1 c. milk
3 tbsp. melted butter

Mix all ingredients. Pour into buttered loaf pan. Bake at 375 degrees for 30 minutes. Serve warm or cold.

PENNSYLVANIA POTATO PANCAKES

2 med. potatoes, peeled
1 tbsp. lemon juice
1/4 c. butter or margarine, melted
2 tbsp. all-purpose flour
1/4 c. finely chopped onion
1 tbsp. thinly sliced scallions
1 lg. egg, beaten
1/2 tsp. salt

1/4 tsp. black pepper
1 tbsp. vegetable oil, or as needed
1 tbsp. butter or margarine, or as needed
1/4 tsp. baking powder

Using coarsest side of hand grater, grate potatoes into large bowl. Toss with lemon juice to coat thoroughly; let stand 5 minutes. Drain well. Add melted butter, flour, onion, scallions, egg, salt, pepper and baking powder to potatoes. Mix well. Heat 1 tablespoon each of oil and butter over medium-high heat. Add potato mixture in heaping tablespoonfuls to skillet; using tines of fork flatten each portion into a thin round. Cook 3-4 minutes on each side. Yields: about 16 pancakes.

SIMPLE DUMPLINGS

1 cup of butter
2 cups eggs about 12
4 1/2 cups of all purpose flour
1 tbsp. baking powder
1/4 tsp. salt
4 sprigs of parsley finely chopped

3 large carrots peeled and sliced

1 cup of green beans cut to preference

2 1/2 cups of shredded chicken

large pot of chicken broth or stock

Preparation:

1. Beat butter until fluffy
2. Add eggs slowly
3. Add dry ingredients and mix until thoroughly blended (don't over-mix it)
4. Flour your hands and form balls slightly larger than golf balls. lay them on a greased tray
5. Make broth and boil sliced carrots and green beans until soft
6. Add parsley and chicken
7. Bring the soup to a rolling boil and carefully spoon in the dumplings
8. Put on the lid and cook for 10-15 minutes or until soft and fluffy. Do NOT open the lid!
9. Do not overcook them or they will fall apart.

BORSCHT

Editor's Note: This is more traditionally a Mennonite dish.

Splash of olive oil or pat of butter

1 large onion, chopped

1 pound of cubed or shredded beef. Leftover roast is perfect.

12 cups beef stock or broth

1/2 cup of tomato paste

6 large beets

4 large carrots

2 large potatoes

2 cups of shredded cabbage

1 28 ounce can of diced tomatoes

Juice of 1 lime

Salt and pepper to taste

Sour cream, chopped green onions for garnish

Preparation:

1. Roast whole beets, peeled carrots and quartered potatoes on a tray brushed with olive oil and dusted with sea salt at 375 degrees for 45 minutes to an hour or until soft. Once they

cool down you can peel off the beet and potato skins, dice them and slice the carrots. Beets, potatoes and carrots should be soft to your taste and ready to eat.

2. Sautee shredded cabbage with a dollop of butter until soft then leave on the side

3. Heat oil or butter in soup pot on medium low heat. Add onions and salt, sauté until onions are soft.

4. Add beef, cook for a few more minutes.

5. Add the beef broth or stock and the tomato paste except garnish, beets and carrots. Bring to a boil, then reduce flame and let simmer covered for 20 minutes then let it rest.

6. Add the sautéed cabbage, and the roasted beets, potatoes and carrots to the soup, bring to a boil and let simmer for 5 minutes.

7. If you prefer a creamy texture for the borscht, you can use an immersion blender to puree the soup.

8. After simmering for 5 minutes turn off the heat, wait 5 minutes for it to cool slightly before adding a dollop of sour cream. Serve sprinkled with chopped green onions or chives. Do not stir the sour cream in, as makes a nice visual contrast to the rich color of the soup.

BEAN SOUP

1/2 lb. beans
water
3 large potatoes
3 carrots
1 cup broccoli florets
1 cup cauliflower
2 cloves garlic
1 small red onion
2 cubes chicken bouillon
1 cup shredded cheddar cheese
salt, to taste

Soak beans in cold water, drain. Fill saucepan with water to cover beans plus about 2". Bring to boil. Cook for 30 minutes or so, stirring occasionally. As the beans cook, mash some against the side of the pot to add to creaminess of soup. While the beans are cooking, peel and chop potatoes in 1/2" cubes. Cook potatoes with added salt in soup pot with enough water to cover. Chop carrots in small pieces and add to potatoes halfway through cooking. Add broccoli, cauliflower, garlic and onion to potatoes when they test done with a fork. At the same time, add beans and bean broth to potatoes. Add chicken bouillon cubes and shredded cheddar cheese. Simmer all together for 10-15 minutes.

AMISH CHILI SOUP RECIPE

1 pound hamburger

1 onion, diced

1 cup diced celery

1/2 cup carrots

1 can pork and beans

1 can kidney beans

1 can tomato soup

1/2 cup ketchup

1 can lima beans

Corn, if desired

1 handful spaghetti

Fry hamburger with onion in large pan. At same time, boil carrots, celery and spaghetti until vegetables are soft; drain. Add pork and beans, kidney beans, tomato soup, ketchup and limas; add to meat mixture. Season with salt and pepper. Heat through, then serve. If too thick, add tomato juice or water.

CHEDDAR MEATLOAF

Mix together

1 lb lean hamburger

1/2 c diced onion

1 c grated Amish cheddar cheese

3/4 c milk

1/2 c oatmeal

1 egg

Form into a loaf and put in loaf pan
Bake at 400 for 40 mins. Top evenly with sauce (below), return to oven and bake 15 mins longer or until done.

Mix well

2/3 c catsup

1 1/2tsp mustard

1/2 c brown sugar

dash of vinegar

CHICKEN DISH

chicken cut up
butter for frying
2 tablespoons flour
2 tablespoons butter
boiled rice
2 cups water
12 small white onions
small pinch each of thyme,
celery salt and sage

Roll chicken pieces in flour and brown in butter. Add remaining ingredients and cook until tender, adding water so that there are 2 cups at end of cooking. Make gravy by adding 3 tablespoons of hot liquid to yolk of an egg. Stir thoroughly, then return to rest of liquid and cook five minutes. Pour over steamed rice

MEAT PIE

1 1/2 cups leftover meat

3 tbsp. flour

1/4 cup drippings

1 cup milk

1 tbsp. grated onion

1/3 cup chopped pepper

salt

pepper

Add flour to drippings and blend, add milk gradually and cook, stirring constantly until it thickens. Stir in the salt, onion and green pepper. Mix cut-up meat into the gravy and pour it into pastry lined baking dish. Top with crust and bake in hot oven (425-f) for 25 minutes.

HAM POTATO CASSEROLE

1/2 cup chopped onion

1 tbsp oil

1 cups milk

4 or 5 potatoes, peeled and sliced

2 cups cubed ham

1 lb fresh string beans (or 1 package frozen)

4 oz shredded Cheddar cheese, optional

Place sliced potatoes in a 13x9 baking dish, add beans and ham. In a saute pan, cook the onion in the oil until it's tender, place in baking dish. Pour milk over all. Cover and place in a 350 degree oven for about 45 minutes. Check beans and potatoes for doneness. If not done, bake about 15 minutes more. Uncover and add cheese if you want and bake about 5 minutes more, until the cheese melts.

BAKED NOODLES WITH HAM

6–8 oz noodles, cooked and drained

3 tbsp butter

3 tbsp flour

1 tbsp mustard

1 1/2 cups milk

2 cups cooked ham, chopped fine or shredded

1 cup celery, chopped fine

salt and pepper to taste

bread crumbs

dots of butter

Combine butter, flour and mustard in saucepan. Add milk gradually, stirring constantly, cook until thick. Add ham, salt, pepper and celery, then stir in the noodles. Pour into greased baking dish. Sprinkle with bread crumbs and dot with butter over the whole mixture. Bake at 350 degrees for 30-45 minutes.

CHICKEN POT PIE

Pot Pie Dough:
3 c. flour
2 eggs
1 Tbsp. shortening
1/2–3/4 c. water

Chicken Broth:
3 lb. whole chicken
2 quarts of water
4–6 medium potatoes
2 c. diced celery
1 c. diced carrots
1 small diced onion
parsley to taste
salt & pepper to taste

To prepare pot pie dough: combine flour, eggs, and shortening. Knead it with your hands adding water small amounts at a time until the dough holds together. Roll out into a thin sheet on a floured board. Cut into 2 inch squares, and let dry about an hour. Meanwhile, cook chicken in 2 quarts of water until tender. Cool and debone and set aside.

Add all remaining chicken mixture ingredients to boiling broth and cook about 10 minutes. Drop pot pie squares into boiling broth a few at a time, turn heat down to medium, stir frequently. Add chicken to broth, heat through.

HOMEMADE MEATBALLS

1 lb. ground beef

1 egg

1/4 c. minced onion

2 Tbsp. ketchup

1/8 tsp. garlic powder

1/8 tsp. italian seasoning

1 tsp. oregano

2 tsp. basil

salt & pepper to taste

8 oz. shredded mozzarella

2 1/4 Tbsp. parmesan cheese

6 Tbsp. bread crumbs

28 oz. jar spaghetti sauce

Combine ground beef and egg. Mix together. Add onion, ketchup and seasonings, mix well. Add cheeses and bread crumbs and mix well again. Shape into balls and cook with spaghetti sauce until done.

SWEET AND SOUR MEATBALLS

1 lb. sausage

2 lbs. ground beef

1 1/2 c. bread crumbs

1 or 2 eggs (depending how dry)

1/8 tsp. nutmeg

1/8 tsp. garlic salt

1 med. onion chopped

1/4 c. milk

Sauce:

1/2 c. sugar

1/2 c. vinegar

1/3 c. pineapple juice

1/4 c. ketchup

1 Tbsp. soy sauce

3 Tbsp. cornstarch

3 Tbsp. water

1 med. green pepper chopped

15 1/4 oz. can pineapple chunks

Mix meatball ingredients, and shape into balls. Bake at 325 degrees for 15-20 minutes. In a large pan, combine sugar, vinegar, pineapple juice, ketchup and soy sauce, and bring to a boil. Combine cornstarch and water and stir into sauce. Add pineapple chunks and green pepper and heat through, stirring often. Add meatballs to sauce.

MENNONITE MEATBALLS

3/4 pound ground pork

3/4 pound ground beef

1 onion, chopped finely

Salt and pepper

3/4 cup rice, soaked in water

2 eggs

1 cup breadcrumbs

1 cup catsup or tomato sauce

Mix all but the catsup and form into balls; brown balls in a pan, put in an oven dish and cover with blended catsup and 1 quart of boiling water. Let simmer in oven for 3 to 4 hours, making sure the balls haven't gone dry.

MENNONITE BROWN FLOUR POTATO SOUP

6 medium potatoes

3 cups water

3 cups milk

3 tablespoons flour

3 tablespoons butter

Salt, pepper and parsley

Peel and cut potatoes in slices. Boil them in salted water until tender. Add the milk and let simmer.

Meanwhile brown the flour in the melted butter, stirring all the time over low heat; add it to the soup, stirring until the mixture thickens. Sprinkle with parsley and pepper.

Serve with buttered crumbs, or squares of fried bread, or pretzels on top. You might boil some sliced onion with the potatoes, if you like.

LIVER BARBECUE

Editor's Note: Admittedly maybe not the most appetizing sounding recipe!

1/2 cup tomato juice

1/4 cup water

2 tablespoons apple cider vinegar

2 tablespoons ketchup

1 tablespoon Worcestershire sauce

1 tablespoon brown sugar

1/2 teaspoon salt

1/2 teaspoon dry mustard

1/8 teaspoon chili powder

2 tablespoons bacon drippings

1 pound beef liver

Combine first 9 ingredients in small saucepan. Simmer for 15 minutes, stirring occasionally.

Remove any veins or skin from liver. Cut into 1/2-inch strips.

Heat bacon drippings in large skillet. Add liver strips, stirring constantly over high heat, just until the meat loses its red color. Overcooking makes liver tough.

Stir the barbecue sauce into the skillet containing the liver. Simmer together only until piping hot. Serve over rice or noodles. Makes 4 servings

CHICKEN CORN & RIVEL SOUP

3 to 4 pound stewing chicken

2 tablespoons salt

1/4 teaspoon pepper

1-1/2 cups celery, chopped

1 medium onion, chopped

2 tablespoons minced parsley

1 quart corn, fresh, frozen, or canned

Hard-boiled eggs, chopped, optional

Chopped parsley, optional

Rivels

In large kettle cover chicken with water. Add salt and pepper. Cook until soft. Remove bones and skin from chicken and cut meat into small pieces.

Heat broth to boiling point and add remaining ingredients. Cook about 15 minutes. Add meat. Heat thoroughly. Garnish with hard-boiled egg or parsley.

RIVELS

1 cup flour
1 egg
1/4 cup milk

Combine flour and egg. Add milk. Mix rivels by cutting with two forks to make crumbs the size of cherry stones. Drop rivels into boiling broth while stirring to prevent rivels from packing together. Makes 8 to 10 servings

CHICKEN DRESSING CASSEROLE

1 (14.5 ounce) can chicken broth
1 stick unsalted butter
1 cup water
2 tablespoons chicken base or bouillon granules
1 cup milk
3 eggs

1 (1-pound) loaf white bread, cubed, toasted
2 cups cooked, cubed chicken
3 ribs celery, diced
3 carrots, shredded
1 onion, diced
1/4 cup chopped parsley
1 teaspoon seasoning salt
1/4 teaspoon freshly ground pepper
1/4 teaspoon salt
1/4 teaspoon celery seed

Preheat oven to 350 degrees.

Combine broth, butter, water, and chicken base in a small saucepan over medium heat until butter is melted and base is dissolved; let cool completely. Whisk in milk and eggs.

Mix together bread cubes, chicken, celery, carrots, onion, parsley, seasoning salt, pepper, salt and celery seed in a large bowl. Pour broth mixture over; toss until liquid is absorbed.

Place dressing mixture into a 13 x 9-inch baking pan. Bake until golden brown, about 1 hour and 20 minutes. Makes 10 servings

COLD DAY SOUP

1 large carrot

2 cups water

2 large onions

1 quart diced potatoes

2 tablespoons rice

1/3 cup macaroni

1 teaspoon salt

1/4 teaspoon pepper

2 cups milk

2 tablespoons flour

Chop carrot and cook in 2 cups water. While cooking, chop onions.

When carrot is partially cooked add onions, potatoes, rice, macaroni, salt and pepper. Add enough water to cover and cook until tender.

Add milk and butter and heat thoroughly.

HOMEMADE CORN CHOWDER

3 pieces salt pork, sliced

4 potatoes, sliced

6 soda crackers, soaked in milk

1 cup milk

1 teaspoon salt

1 onion, sliced

2 cups water

2 cups corn

1/4 teaspoon paprika

Cut the salt pork in cubes and brown. Add onion and cook until browned; add the potatoes and water and cook until potatoes are soft.

When potatoes are cooked, stir in the crackers which have been soaked in the milk, corn, salt and paprika. Heat thoroughly and serve.

GARDEN VEGGIE SOUP

2 tablespoons butter

1 onion, chopped

1 pound hamburger

1-1/2 teaspoon salt

1 cup carrots, diced

1/2 cup celery, chopped

1 cup potatoes, diced

2 cups tomato juice

2 cups milk

1/4 cup flour

Brown meat and onion in butter. Add remaining ingredients, except milk and flour, and cook until vegetables are tender.

Combine milk and flour to stir until smooth. Add to soup and cook until thickened. Makes 4-6 servings.

SWISS MEATLOAF

1 egg

1/2 cup evaporated milk

1/2 teaspoon rubbed sage

1 teaspoon salt

1/2 teaspoon black pepper

1-1/2 pounds lean ground beef

1 cup Ritz cracker crumbs

3/4 cup grated Swiss cheese

1/4 cup finely chopped onion

2 to 3 strips bacon, cut into 1-inch pieces

Preheat oven to 350 degrees.

Beat the egg in a large bowl. Add evaporated milk, sage, salt and pepper; mix well. Add beef, crumbs, 1/2 cup of the cheese and the onion; blend together.

Form into a loaf and place in a 2-quart rectangular baking dish. Arrange bacon pieces on top of loaf.

Bake at 350 degrees for 40 minutes. Sprinkle with remaining cheese on top and bake 10 minutes longer, or until done.

AMISH POURED NOODLE SOUP

2 quarts seasoned chicken broth

3 eggs

1/4 cup milk

1 teaspoon salt

3/4 cup flour

Bring broth to boiling in a large pot.
Beat together eggs and milk. Stir in salt and flour. Pour batter from bowl into boiling broth in a thin string. Keep the broth boiling. After the last of the batter has been added, there is no need to boil any longer. The soup is done.

HUSBAND'S DELIGHT

24 ounces tomato sauce

1/2 cup sour cream

1 cup cottage cheese

8 ounces cream cheese

1 medium onion, chopped fine

1 cup grated Cheddar cheese

1 1/2 pounds ground beef

1/4 cup bell pepper, chopped

2 cloves garlic, chopped

1 (8 ounce) package wide noodles, cooked as directed

1 tablespoon granulated sugar

Brown ground beef, bell peppers, and garlic together and drain. Cook noodles as directed then drain. Add noodles, sugar, and tomato sauce to ground beef. Stir. Combine sour cream, cottage cheese, cream cheese and onion. Put into a 3-quart casserole dish a layer of noodles and meat, then a layer of cheese mixture; add the remaining meat and noodle mixture. Add grated cheese. Bake at 350 degrees F for 25 to 30 minutes. Yields 10 to 12 servings.

LAYERED DINNER

2 cups hamburger (uncooked)

2 cups sliced raw potatoes

2 cups chopped celery

1/2 cup diced onions

2 teaspoons salt

1/4 teaspoon pepper

1 cup diced green pepper

2 cups canned tomatoes

1 onion, thinly sliced (optional)

Preheat oven to 350 degrees F.

Grease a casserole dish Sprinkle each layer with salt and pepper before adding the next layer. Place potatoes in the bottom of the casserole dish. Add layer of celery. Add layer of hamburger Add the layer of onions. Add the green pepper. Pour the tomatoes over the mixture. Lay onion slices on top, if desired. Bake for 2 hours, covering with foil after about one hour.

HOMEMADE BOLOGNA

3 pounds hamburger

3 tablespoons Morton's Tender Quick

1 cup water

1/8 teaspoon garlic powder

1/2 teaspoon onion powder

1 1/2 teaspoons Liquid Smoke

Mix well. Roll into 2 rolls. Wrap in plastic wrap; put in refrigerator 24 hours.

Put on greased pan. Bake 1 hour at 300 degrees F, turning meat once halfway through baking time.

PLAIN DUMPLINGS

1 cup of butter
2 cups eggs about 12
4 1/2 cups of all purpose flour
1 tbsp. baking powder
1/4 tsp. salt
4 sprigs of parsley finely chopped
3 large carrots peeled and sliced
1 cup of green beans cut to preference
2 1/2 cups of shredded chicken
large pot of chicken broth or stock

Preparation:
1. Beat butter until fluffy
2. Add eggs slowly
3. Add dry ingredients and mix until thoroughly blended (don't over-mix it)
4. Flour your hands and form balls slightly larger than golf balls. lay them on a greased tray
5. Make broth and boil sliced carrots and green beans until soft

6. Add parsley and chicken
7. Bring the soup to a rolling boil and carefully spoon in the dumplings
8. Put on the lid and cook for 10-15 minutes or until soft and fluffy. Do NOT open the lid!
9. Do not overcook them or they will fall apart.

SIDE DISHES

ZUCCHINI POTATO PATTIES

1 1/2 cups shredded potatoes

1 1/2 cups zucchini, shredded

1/4 cup onions (diced)

2 tablespoons flour

1 teaspoon salt

1/2 teaspoon pepper

3 eggs (slightly beaten)

Fry until golden brown.

FRIED SUMMER SQUASH

Use yellow squash.

Slice thinly and salt them. In olive oil in a frying pan, fry garlic slices and fresh basil leaves until brown. In another frypan in olive oil fry the squash slices that have been floured. Fry until golden brown on both sides. Eat hot.

ZUCCHINI PATTIES

2 cups peeled, shredded zucchinis
1 teaspoon salt
1 1/2 tablespoons flour
18 Saltine crackers, crushed
2 eggs, beaten

Mix all ingredients together. Shape into patties with spoon and fry in butter.

CREAMY COLE SLAW

1 head cabbage
1/2 cup chopped onions
2 medium carrots, shredded
1 cup cheddar cheese
1 cup tomatoes, chopped

Dressing:
1 cup white sugar
1/3 cup Ranch dressing
1 cup sour cream
1/2 teaspoon salt
1 cup salad dressing

Mix first 5 ingredients and stir in dressing. Put into serving dish and top with shredded cheese.

BROCCOLI RAMEN SALAD

Editor's Note: this recipe may be tied with the curly fry casserole as one of the most unusual submissions! This recipe came from the Amish settlement of Choteau, Oklahoma.

1 1/2 – 2 pounds fresh broccoli, cut in florets

2 large red peppers, cut into large chunks

1/2 cup butter, divided

1 head lettuce, chopped

2 cups pecans, chopped

3 packages Ramen noodles, chicken flavored

Fill fix and mix a bowl half full with broccoli. Fill up with lettuce and peppers. Toast pecans in 1/4 cup butter over low heat till golden, stirring occasionally. Sprinkle with salt while toasting. Cool. Toast ramen noodles in remaining butter till golden, stirring occasionally. Cool. Toss in with salad. Add dressing just before serving.

Dressing: 2 cups sugar, 2 cups oil, 2/3 cup red wine vinegar, 3 packages of seasoning from noodles.

AMISH SLAW

1 medium head cabbage, cored and shredded

1 medium onion, finely chopped

1 cup white sugar

1 cup vinegar

1 teaspoon salt

1 teaspoon celery seed

1 teaspoon white sugar

1 teaspoon prepared mustard

3/4 cup vegetable oil

In a large bowl, toss together the cabbage, onion, and 1 cup sugar. In a small saucepan, combine the vinegar, salt, celery seed, 1 teaspoon white sugar, mustard and oil. Bring to a boil, and cook for 3 minutes. Cool completely, then pour over cabbage mixture, and toss to coat. Refrigerate overnight for best flavor.

AMISH HONEY CARROTS WITH SWEET PICKLES

1 lb. carrots

3 tbsp. butter

1/4 c. honey

1/4 c. orange juice

1/2 tsp. grated orange rind

1/2 tsp. salt

1/2 tsp. ginger

1/4 tsp. black pepper

3 tbsp. chopped sweet pickle

Peel carrots and slice; melt butter in skillet. Add all ingredients except sweet pickles. Cover and cook about 20 minutes, stirring occasionally. Uncover, raise heat to high and cook about 3 minutes to reduce the sauce to glaze. Stir in pickles just before serving.

AMISH BAKED BEANS

1 lb. navy beans

1/2 lb. bacon ends

1 med. onion (quartered)

1/4 c. brown sugar

1/3 c. molasses

2 tsp. dry mustard

2 tsp. salt

1/4 tsp. pepper

2 tbsp. vinegar

2 c. hot water

Long cooking develops the wonderful old-fashioned flavor. Soak beans overnight in 6 cups water; add 1/4 teaspoon baking soda if water is hard. Parboil beans for 20 minutes. Drain beans after parboiling; rinse with cold water. Dice bacon ends to 1 inch square, placing half in the bottom of a 2 quart bean pot or casserole along with the quartered onion. Add beans. Mix remaining ingredients with hot water. Pour over top of beans. Top with remaining bacon ends. Cover and bake in a slow (300 degree) oven for about 6 hours adding hot water as needed to keep beans moist. Serves 8 to 10.

AMISH TURNIPS

2 c. cooked turnips
2/3 c. bread crumbs
1 tbsp. oleo or margarine
2 tbsp. brown sugar
1 c. milk
1 egg
Salt and pepper

Cook turnips until tender. Drain, mash and then add 1/2 cup bread crumbs, saving rest for top. Add egg, sugar, milk, salt and pepper to taste. Mix together; pour into greased baking dish. Dot with butter and rest of crumbs. Bake 45 minutes at 375 degrees

AMISH CHICKEN DRESSING

1/2 c. finely chopped onion
1/2 c. finely chopped celery
1/2 c. finely chopped carrots
1 c. diced potatoes
1/2 c. margarine
1 c. chicken broth

Cook until vegetables are tender. 1 large loaf dried bread cut into cubes. 1 tsp. salt 1/8 tsp. pepper 1 c. milk 1 c. chicken broth 2 c. finely chopped chicken, cooked Add to vegetable mixture and mix thoroughly. Add more broth if necessary. Bake 35–45 minutes at 350 degrees.

MENNONITE RED CABBAGE

2 tbsp. cooking oil

4 c. shredded red cabbage

2 c. unpared cubed apples

1/4 c. brown sugar

1/4 c. vinegar

1/4 c. water

1/2 tsp. caraway seed

Salt and pepper

In skillet, heat oil. Add remaining ingredients. Cover and cook over low heat, stirring occasionally. Cook 25–30 minutes. Garnish with apple wedges, if desired.

KRAUT CASSEROLE

1 lb. sauerkraut

1 c. sugar

6 slices bacon

1 tsp. black pepper

Mix sauerkraut, pepper and sugar together in 1-1/2 quart dish. Cut bacon slices in 1 inch pieces and mix slightly with sauerkraut. Bake at 325 degrees for 2-1/4 hours

DANDELION SALAD

Young dandelion greens

4 thick slices bacon

1/2 cup cream

2 tbsp. butter

2 eggs

1 tsp. salt

1 tbsp. sugar

4 tbsp. vinegar

1/2 tsp. paprika

black pepper

Wash dandelions and pick over carefully. Roll in cloth and pat dry. Put into a salad bowl and set in warm place. Cut bacon in small cubes, fry quickly and pour over dandelions. Put butter and cream into a skillet and melt over low heat. Beat eggs, add salt, pepper, sugar and vinegar, then mix with the slightly warm cream mixture. Cook over high heat until dressing is quite thick. Pour, very hot, over the dandelions, stir well and serve.

HOT POTATO SALAD

4 slices bacon

1/2 cup chopped onion

1/2 cup chopped green pepper

1/4 cup vinegar

1 teaspoon salt

3 hard boiled eggs

1/8 teaspoon pepper

1 teaspoon sugar

1 egg

1 qt. hot, cubed, cooked potatoes

1/4 cup grated raw carrot

Dice bacon and pan fry. Add chopped onion and green pepper. Cook 3 minutes. Add vinegar, salt, pepper, sugar and beaten egg. Cook slightly. Add cubed potatoes, grated carrot and diced hard-cooked eggs. Blend and serve hot.

BREAD FILLING

6 med. potatoes

2 ribs celery, chopped fine

1 sm. Onion, chopped fine

1 c. bread cubes (I buy bread already cubed for stuffing)

butter (don't be shy with it)

1 tbsp. parsley

1 egg, optional

Boil potatoes, mash and set aside. In a large saute pan, melt butter and saute onion and celery until almost soft. Add the bread cubes and cook until vegetables are done. If you want add a bit more butter, the filling is really good with buttery bread cubes. Add bread, onion and celery and parsley to mashed potatoes and mix well. Sometimes for a different flavor, add a peeled clove of garlic or two into the potatoes as they boil. It gets mashed up, and enhances the flavor. It is not original to the dish.

MENNONITE RED CABBAGE AND APPLE SALAD

4 cups shredded red cabbage

1 cup apples, quartered and sliced thin

1 teaspoon salt

2 tablespoons brown sugar

2 tablespoons vinegar

3 tablespoons butter

1/2 teaspoon mustard

1/2 cup sour cream

Pepper

Melt the butter in a saucepan. Add the cabbage and apple and stir until the butter coats the mixture and there are signs of softening, but the mixture is not really cooked. Add the vinegar, sugar, seasonings and mustard; simmer another 2 minutes, then stir in the sour cream. Serve hot.

HOT POTATO SALAD WITH BACON

4 slices lean bacon
1/2 cup finely chopped onions
1/4 cup chopped celery
1 tablespoon flour
1/4 cup hot water
1/2 cup heavy cream
2 tablespoon boiled dressing
1 tablespoon vinegar
1/2 teaspoon salt
1/4 teaspoon freshly ground pepper
4 cups diced, hot, boiled potatoes
1 tablespoon finely chopped parsley
1 teaspoon finely chopped chives
Additional heavy cream (optional)
2 hard-boiled eggs, sliced

Cook bacon over medium heat until crisp. Remove and crumble. Drain off all fat except 1 tablespoon, return to medium heat, add onions and celery. Stir in flour to coat the vegetable. Add water, stir and cook till thickened. Remove from the heat and blend in the cream, boiled dressing, vinegar, salt, and pepper. Pour over the potatoes in a large bowl. Add the parsley and chives. Mix well to blend flavors. Add more cream if desired, taste, add salt if desired. Sprinkle crumbled bacon on top and garnish with the sliced hard-boiled eggs.

GERMAN SUMMER SALAD

2 cups raw spinach, finely chopped

1 thinly sliced peeled cucumber

4 green onions, chopped

1/2 cup sliced radishes

2 cups cottage cheese

1 cup sour cream

2 teaspoons fresh or bottled lemon juice

1/2 teaspoon salt

1/4 teaspoon freshly ground pepper

Paprika, to taste

1/2 cup minced fresh parsley

Wash the spinach the day before, then wrap it in a cloth and refrigerate it overnight.

Chop the spinach, add the cucumber, onions and radishes, then toss lightly. Arrange in a wooden salad bowl and place a mound of cottage cheese in the middle.

Blend the sour cream with the lemon juice, salt and pepper and pour over the salad. Sprinkle the paprika in the middle and the parsley all around. Toss when ready to serve.

SLAW

1 cup vinegar

1/2 cup vegetable oil

1/4 cup water

1 teaspoon mustard

1 teaspoon celery seed

1 teaspoon sugar

1 1/2 teaspoons salt

1 medium cabbage

2 medium onions

1 cup granulated sugar

Mix vinegar, oil, water, mustard, celery seed, sugar and salt; boil for 3 minutes. Mix cabbage, onions and sugar. Combine boiled mixture and cabbage mixture; refrigerate overnight.

AUNT MAUDIE'S BROWN BUTTER RECIPE

For each four servings of vegetable, melt 1/2 cup butter slowly. Allow it to brown until it is almost black. Pour over vegetables.

BREAD FILLING

4 eggs

2 cups milk

2 quarts soft bread cubes

4 tablespoons melted butter

1 tablespoon parsley, chopped

1 teaspoon onion, minced

1 teaspoon salt

1 teaspoon sage or poultry seasoning

Beat eggs. Add milk. Pour over bread cubes.

Combine butter and seasonings. Add to bread cubes and mix well.

Filling can be baked in a casserole dish at 350 degrees for 45 minutes or may be used as stuffing for fowl. Makes 6 servings

SMASHED TURNIPS

2 cups cooked turnips

2/3 cup bread crumbs

1 tablespoon butter or margarine

2 tablespoons brown sugar

1 cup milk

1 egg

Salt and pepper, to taste

Cook turnips until tender. Drain and mash them; add 1/2 cup bread crumbs, reserving remainder for top.

Add egg, sugar, milk, salt and pepper, to taste. Mix together, pour into greased baking dish. Dot with butter a0nd remaining bread crumbs. Bake 45 minutes at 375 degrees.

SCALLOPED CELERY AND CHEESE

Editor's Note: Celery and cheese? Seems an odd combination!

3 cups celery, diced

1 tablespoon butter

3 tablespoons flour

1-1/2 cups milk

1/2 cup celery liquid

3/4 teaspoon salt

Dash of pepper

1 cup grated cheese

1 cup buttered crumbs

Cook celery in water until tender. Drain, reserving 1/2 cup of liquid.

Melt butter. Add flour and stir until smooth. Gradually add milk and celery liquid. Cook, stirring constantly until thickened. Add salt, pepper, and cheese. Stir until cheese melts.

In greased casserole, place a layer of celery, then cheese sauce, then buttered crumbs. Repeat, ending with crumbs. Bake at 350 degrees for 30 to 40 minutes. Makes 6 servings

SWEET POTATO PUDDING

2 cups mashed sweet potatoes

3 tablespoons sugar

2 eggs, well beaten

2 tablespoons melted butter

1 teaspoon salt

1 cup milk

1/2 cup miniature marshmallows or marshmallow créme

Combine all ingredients except marshmallows. Blend well.

Pour into buttered casserole. Top with marshmallows. Bake at 350 degrees for 45 minutes. Makes 4 to 6 servings

TOMATO FRITTERS

1 c. all-purpose flour

1 tsp. sugar

1/4 tsp. dried basil OR

2 tbsp. fresh basil, minced

1 tbsp. parsley, minced

1 egg

Vegetable oil for frying

1 tsp. baking powder

3/4 tsp. salt

1 (28 oz.) can tomatoes, drained

1 tbsp. onions, minced

1/2 tsp. Worcestershire sauce

In a large bowl, combine flour, baking powder, sugar, basil and salt. Cut tomatoes into 1/2 inch pieces and drain further on a paper towel. Add them to the flour mixture along with onion, parsley and Worcestershire sauce, but do not mix in. In small bowl, beat egg and add it to the flour-tomato mixture. Blend lightly with a fork. Heat oil (about 1/4 inch) in fry pan. Drop the batter by tablespoons into hot oil. Fry until golden brown on both sides. Keep fritters warm in oven until serving. Serves 4 - 6.

PIES, CAKES & BREADS

SPICE CAKE

1 cup vegetable oil

2 cups brown sugar

4 eggs

2 teaspoons baking soda

1 teaspoon salt

2 teaspoons cinnamon

4 cups grated carrots

2 cups flour

1 teaspoon nutmeg

1/2 teaspoon ginger

1/2 teaspoon cardamom

Mix ingredients in order given. Bake in a floured 9 X 13-inch pan at 325 for 30-35 minutes or until an inserted toothpick comes out clean.

RHURBARB PIE

1 cup rhubarb, cut-up

2 eggs, yolks only

2 tablespoons flour

1 cup sugar

1 cup milk

pinch salt

Put rhubarb in pie shell and pour custard over it and bake. When almost done put whites of eggs on top to brown. Makes 1 pie.

PUMPKIN PIE

1 cup pumpkin (cooked and mashed)

1 cup white sugar

1/2 cup brown sugar

3 egg yolks

4 tablespoons flour

1/4 teaspoons each cinnamon, allspice and nutmeg

1 teaspoon salt

A little lemon flavor

3 cups hot milk

Mix altogether. Then stir in beaten egg whites. Add hot milk. Pour into pie crusts. Makes two pies. May use sweet potatoes or butternut squash instead of pumpkin

MOLASSES COOKIES

3/4 cup oleo
2 1/2 cups brown
3 eggs
1/2 cups molasses
1/2 cup corn syrup
2 teaspoons cinnamon
3 teaspoons baking soda
6 1/2 cups flour

Mix ingredients in the order given. Shape into teaspoon sized balls and roll in sugar. Place on greased cookie sheets. Bake at 350 until golden brown. Do not overbake. Good for sandwich cookies with frosting in between.
Tip: it is important to chill the dough.

EMERGENCY BISCUITS

2 cups flour
1 teaspoon salt
4 teaspoons baking powder
4 teaspoons shortening
1 cup milk

Mix first 4 ingredients well and add milk. Drop onto cookie sheets. Bake at 350 until nice and golden.

ZUCCHINI BREAD

2 cups flour

2 cups sugar

1 teaspoon baking soda

1 teaspoon baking powder

1 teaspoon salt

1 cup vegetable oil

2 cups zucchini (peeled and grated)

1/2 cup nuts

3 eggs

2 teaspoon vanilla

Mix dry ingredients and then the rest; mix well. Bake in moderate oven for 1 hour or until done.

EGGLESS CHOCOLATE CAKE

2 cups white sugar

2 teaspoons baking soda

2 cups sour milk or buttermilk

1/2 cup melted lard, put in loast

1 teaspoon vanilla

3 cups flour

2 tablespoons cocoa

Bake at 350

Variation: omit chocolate and add spices for a spice cake or make a lemon cake.

SWEET DESSERT

Editor's Note: This recipe comes from the Amish settlement around Watsontown, Pennsylvania.

1 box brownie mix

First layer:

1-8 ounce box cream cheese

1 8-oz Cool Whip

1 1/2 cups 10 X sugar

After brownies are baked and cool, add first layer then add second layer:

Second layer:

1 box chocolate pudding mix

1 1/2 cup milk

Mix together till thick. Pour over first mixture then top with 1 -8 ounce Cool Whip.

RASPBERRY ANGEL TORTE

Editor's Note: Recipe from Mrs. Toby Byler outside of Watsontown, Pennsylvania.

1 box cream cheese

1 cup sugar

1 cup 10 X sugar

1 8 ounce Cool Whip

1 angel food cake

In layers then add cream cheese mixture and your flavor of fruit filling, raspberry, cherry or strawberry.

RHUBARB UPSIDE DOWN CAKE

3 eggs, beaten

1 cup sugar

1 1/2 cup melted margarine

3/4 cup sweet milk

3 teaspoons baking powder

2 cups flour

1 teaspoon vanilla

Pinch of salt

2 cups rhubarb

1 cup sugar

1 cup boiling water

Cut and put rhubarb on bottom of pan. Put sugar over rhubarb and then pour boiling water over rhubarb. Do this first then mix cake batter and pour over rhubarb. Bake at 350. Serve warm with milk and sugar if not sweet enough.

BANANA SPLIT PIE

1 cup all-purpose flour

1/2 cup nuts

1 stick margarine

Mix well and spread in a 9 X 13 inch pan. Bake for 15 minutes at 350 and cool.

1st layer:

1 cup Cool Whip

1 cup powdered sugar

1 8 ounce cream cheese

Cream together and spread over crust

2nd layer:

2 cups well drained crushed pineapple

4 or 5 sliced bananas

3rd layer:

12 ounces Cool Whip

Chopped nuts on top of Cool Whip

1 can Cherry Pie filling

Hershey's syrup drizzled over top

Refrigerate 24 hours before serving.

PINEAPPLE BANANA BREAD

3 cups flour

2 cups sugar

1 teaspoon salt

1 tablespoon baking soda

1 teaspoon cinnamon

3 eggs

1 1/4 cup vegetable oil

8 ounces of crushed pineapple, drained

2 cups mashed bananas (4 to 5 medium)

Mix well. Pour into two pans. Bake at 350 for 1 hour.

MISSISSIPPI MUD PIE

1 1/2 cup brown sugar

2 1/2 cups milk

1/2 cup water

1 teaspoon vanilla

3 egg yolks

4 tablespoons flour

12 graham crackers

1 tablespoon butter, heaping

Melt butter and brown sugar. Add sugar and water and boil until thick. Add vanilla and put into a dish. Roll graham crackers and spread on to. Spread with beaten egg white and a few graham cracker crumbs. Brown slightly.

OREO COOKIE DESSERT

Editor's Note: Recipe comes from the large Amish community near Millersburg, Ohio

1 pound Oreo cookies

Crush cookies to form crumbs and reserve 1/4 cup crumbs.
Mix cookie crumbs and 1/2 cup melted butter. Press into 13 X 9 inch pan.

2–3 ounce bozes of vanilla instant pudding
8 ounces cream cheese
3 1/2 cups milk

Mix together and spread on crust top with 4 ounces Cool Whip or whipped topping. Put reserve crumbs on top.

FINNISH COFFECAKE

Editor's Note: This recipe's title perplexed me. Anyone have any ideas as to how this coffeecake got it's Finnish moniker? This recipe came from Dorcas Raber in Flat Rock, Illinois, here is what she wrote with it:

If you are out of eggs, this cake is a dandy. If you are health conscious, add less sugar and substitute vegetable oil for 1/2 cup applesauce and a 1 /2 cup oil. Add 1 cup whole wheat flour ad 1 cup white flour. Or use your own imagination and judgment!

Mix 1 1/4 cup sugar

1 cup vegetable oil

1 cup milk

1 teaspoon vanilla

Add:

2 cups flour

1 teaspoon baking soda

1/2 teaspoon baking powder

1/2 teaspoon salt

Pour into a greased 13 X 9" pan. Sprinkle topping on top of batter: 1/2 cup brown sugar and 1 tablespoon cinnamon.

FRUIT PIZZA

Editor's Note: This recipe comes from Dorcas Raber in Flat Rock, Illinois. Of this recipe she says: "This ranks high in our family!"

Crust: 1 box yellow cake mix

3 /4 cup graham cracker crumbs

3/4 cup flour

1/4 cup white sugar

2 eggs, beaten

3/4 cup butter

1 teaspoon baking soda

Preheat oven to 350. Press batter into a greased 15 X 10" pan. Bake 10 to 12 minutes. Do not overbake. Cool.

Filling: Beat 8 ounces cream cheese. Add 1 /3 cup powdered sugar and 2 cups whipped topping a dash of vanilla. Put on cooled crust. Then top with your choice filling (blueberry, peach, whatever) Or you can top with your favorite fruit glaze and various fresh fruits.

FRUIT-NUT TORTE

2 beaten eggs

1 cup sugar

2 cups drained fruit cocktail

1/2 cup fruit cocktail juice

2 cups flour

1 teaspoon soda

1 1/2 teaspoon salt

Pour batter into a greased 13 X 9 pan. Sprinkle with the following topping:
1/3 cup brown sugar, 1/2 cup chocolate chips

Bake at 350 for 25-30 minutes. Cake should be golden brown.

Boil 3 minutes: 1/3 cup white sugar, 1/3 cup milk, and 4 tablespoons butter
Remove from heat and add 1 teaspoon vanilla. Pour on hot cake.

SWISS ROLL CAKE

Bottom layer:

One chocolate cake mix or favorite chocolate cake recipe. Bake on cookie sheet until done. Cool.

Second layer:

1-8 ounce Cool Whip

1 1/2 cps powdered sugar

1-8 ounce cream cheese

2 tablespoons milk

Mix together and spread on top of cake

Frosting:

5 tablespoons butter, melted

Remove from heat then add 1 ½ cup chocolate chips. Stir until chips are melted. Drizzle over second layer.

CHOCOLATE LOGS

3 cups powdered sugar

1 1/2 cups peanut butter

1 cup melted butter

3 1/2 cups Rice Krispie cereal

1 cup coconut

Mix together all the ingredients. Roll into little logs and put in pan in rows. Melt 2 cups of chocolate coating. Put a layer of chocolate on each log. Put in a cool place till chocolate hardens.

CAKE ROLL

4 egg yolks

4 egg whites

1/4 teaspoon salt

1 cup sugar

1 cup sifted flour

2 teaspoons baking powder

Beat egg whites till frothy, gradually fold 2/3 cup sugar into egg whites an beat till stiff. Beat egg yolks and the 1/3 cup sugar till light. Fold egg yolks and the 1/3 cup sugar till light. Fold egg yolks then dry ingredients into egg whites. Spread evenly on dusted sheet. Bake at 375 for about 12 minutes. When done immediately turn out on moistened, floured towel and roll. When cool unroll and spread with desired filling. This cake is simple and is nearly always perfect.

APPLE DUMPLINGS

6 apples cut in half

1/2 teaspoon salt

2 cups flour

2/3 cup butter

2 1/2 teaspoon baking powder

1/2 cup milk

Sauce:

3 cups brown sugar

1 cup butter

3 cups water

3/4 teaspoon cinnamon

Mix dry ingredients, cut in butter and add milk. Roll out dough to 1/8 inch thick. Cut into squares and wrap each square with 1/2 apple. Pinch corners together. Place on baking sheet and add syrup. Bake at 350 for 30 minutes. Serve with ice cream or milk. Yum! Yum!

COCONUT OATMEAL PIE

Editor's Note: Oatmeal pie is a traditional dessert among many Amish, but this recipe from Miriam Miller in Fredonia, Pennsylvania is the first I've seen with coconut listed as an ingredient. Neat variation!

1 1/2 cups milk (scant)

2 teaspoons oleo

2 /3 white sugar

1 cup brown sugar

2/3 cup coconut

1/2 cup quick oats

1 teaspoon vanilla flavoring

1/8 teaspoon salt

2 beaten eggs

Heat milk and oleo until oleo is melted. Mix the rest of the ingredients in a bowl. Add milk mixture and stir until everything is mixed well. Pour into unbaked 9 inch pie shell. Immediately put into preheated oven and bake at 350 for one hour or until nice and firmly set. Makes 1 pie.

MAPLE NUT ANGEL FOOD CAKE

2 cups egg whites

1/4 cup water

3/4 teaspoons salt

2 teaspoons cream of tartar

2 1/4 cups brown sugar

1/2 teaspoons maple flavoring

1 teaspoon vanilla flavoring

1 1/2 cups flour and 2 tablespoons cornstarch

1/2 cup chopped nuts

Beat together egg whites, water, salt and cream of tartar until fluffy. Add 1 1/4 cup brown sugar and beat until stiff. Stir in flavorings. Sift flour, cornstarch, and 1 cup brown sugar. Gradually fold into egg white mixture and bake at 350 until cake tester comes out dry, approximately one hour. Remove from oven and let cool upside down. Once it has cooled, loosen sides with a table knife and release cake onto a plate. This is a very tasty cake by itself but may be frosted if you so desire. 1 1/3 cup cake flour can be substituted for flour/cornstarch.

CREAM CHEESE LEMON PIE

1 small box lemon pudding and pie filling (not instant)

1-8 ounce cream cheese, softened

1 cup powdered sugar

1-8 ounce Cool Whip

1-9" deep dish baked pie crust

Cook pudding and pie filling according to the directions on the box. Cool. Mix together cream cheese and powdered sugar, add half of cool whip. Mix well. Fold in lemon pudding. Pour into pie crust and top with remaining cool whip.

CHOCOLATE ZUCCHINI CAKE

3 eggs

1 1/2 cups sugar

1 teaspoon vanilla

1/2 cup vegetable oil

2 cups flour

1/3 cup unsweetened cocoa

1 teaspoon baking powder

1 teaspoon baking soda

1 teaspoon cinnamon

1/4 teaspoon salt

3/4 cup buttermilk or sour milk

3 cups coarsely shredded, raw zucchini

Beat eggs until light and fluffy in a large mixing bowl. Gradually beat in sugar and vanilla until thick and light in color. Gradually pour in oil. Beat until combined. Combine flour, cocoa, baking powder, baking soda, cinnamon, and salt.

AMISH COFFEE CAKE

2 c. light brown sugar

2 c. flour

3/4 c. shortening

1 egg

2 tsp. vanilla

1 c. hot coffee

1 tsp. soda

Mix sugar, flour and shortening until lumpy. Do not mix until creamy. Take out 1 cup for topping. Dissolve soda in hot coffee and add to the flour mixture. Also add egg and vanilla. Spread on sheet pan 9x12x2 inch and sprinkle on topping. This is a thin batter. Bake at 325–350 degrees approximately 30 minutes. Sprinkle with powdered sugar after baked.

AMISH LEMON SPONGE

2 1/2 c. sifted cake flour

1 tsp. salt

2/3 c. shortening

1/3 c. cold water (approximately)

FILLING FOR ONE 9" UNCOOKED PIE SHELL:
2 tbsp. butter

1 c. sugar

3 eggs, separated

3 tbsp. flour

1/2 tsp. salt

Lemon juice & rind of 1 lemon

1 1/2 c. hot milk

Measure sifted flour, add salt and sift again. Cut in shortening using a pastry blender or two knifes. Sprinkle with water mixing lightly with fork. press into ball. Makes enough pastry for a 9 inch two crust pie or two shells. Cream butter; add sugar and egg yolks. Beat until light and fluffy. Stir in flour, salt, lemon juice, rind and hot milk. Fold in stiffly beaten egg whites. Bake in 400 degree oven for approximately 40 minutes. Serves 6 at 371 calories per serving.

AMISH PUMPKIN BREAD

3 c. granulated sugar

1 c. vegetable oil

4 eggs, beaten

1 lb. canned pumpkin

3 1/2 c. flour

2/3 c. water

2 tsp. baking soda

2 tsp. salt (scant)

1/2 tsp. ground cloves

1 tsp. EACH: cinnamon, allspice and nutmeg

Mix sugar, oil and eggs together. Add pumpkin. Then add dry ingredient and finally water, stirring just until mixed. Pour batter into two (2) greased and floured 9x5 inch loaf pans. Bake at 350 degrees for one (1) hour. Especially good spread with cream cheese.

AMISH MUFFINS

5 c. flour

5 tsp. soda

2 tsp. salt

2 tsp. allspice

15 oz. raisin bran

3 c. sugar

Mix above ingredients. Add: 1 c. oil 1 qt. buttermilk 2 tsp. vanilla Mix well. Butter muffin tins well and fill 3/4 full. Bake at 375 degrees for 20 minutes.

AMISH DOUBLE CINNAMON SOURDOUGH BREAD

1 cup Amish Friendship Bread Starter

1 cup vegetable oil

1 cup white sugar

4 eggs

2 teaspoons vanilla extract

2 teaspoons baking soda

1 teaspoon baking powder

1 (3 ounce) package instant vanilla pudding mix

2 cups all-purpose flour

2 teaspoons ground cinnamon

1 cup chopped pecans

1 cup peeled, cored and chopped apple

1 cup raisins

Preheat oven to 325 degrees F (165 degrees C). Grease three 9×5 inch loaf pans.

Place the starter in a bowl, stir in the oil, sugar, eggs and vanilla and mix well.

Combine the flour, baking soda, baking powder, instant pudding, and cinnamon. Add the flour mixture to the starter mixture and beat by hand. Add the pecans, raisins and apples and mix well. Pour batter into the prepared pans. Bake at 325 degrees F (165 degrees C) for 1 hour.

HOMEMADE PENNSLVANIA SHOOFLY PIE

Crumb Topping:

4 cups flour

1 cup brown sugar

1/2 tsp. mixed spices (salt, cloves, nutmeg, ginger, mace)

1/2 cup shortening (NO BUTTER)

Syrup Filling:

1 cup uncultured baking molasses

1 cup boiling water

1 tsp. baking soda

3 eggs

Combine the crumb topping ingredients to form a crumb mixture for pie topping.

Dissolve baking soda in boiling water; add molasses and eggs. Stir and let cool. Have two 9-inch unbaked pastry shells ready. Pour syrup filling into crusts, dividing portions equally. Sprinkle crumb topping over syrup mixture, dividing equally between the two shells. Bake at 375°F for 1 hour.

MENNONITE BREAD PUDDING

2 eggs, well beaten

1/2 cup granulated sugar

2 cups milk

1/4 teaspoon nutmeg, ground

4 cups day old bread (1/2-inch slices), cubed

1/4 cup raisins

Beat eggs. Add sugar, milk and nutmeg. Butter a 1 1/2-quart baking dish. Put bread cubes into dish and pour egg mixture over the bread. Let the bread cubes become soaked by the mixture.

Mix in the raisins. Bake at 350 degrees F for 25 minutes.

MENNONITE MAPLE WALNUT CAKE

1/3 cup soft butter or regular margarine

2 eggs

1 cup maple syrup

1 1/4 cups all-purpose white flour

2 teaspoons baking powder

Pinch salt

1 cup walnuts, chopped not too fine

Beat together butter, eggs, and syrup. This will look curdled don't worry. Sift together flour, baking powder, and salt, and stir in gradually.
Beat with whisk until smooth fold in walnuts.

Pour into a greased square pan and bake at 350 degrees F for about 25 to 30 minutes or until done. Let cool before icing with a maple butter icing.

Maple Butter Icing:
Melt 2 tablespoons butter, blend in a cupful of sifted icing sugar and moisten to a spreading consistency with maple syrup.

MENNONITE OATMEAL CAKE

1 c. quick rolled oats

1 1/2 c. boiling water

1/2 c. butter or margarine

1 c. brown sugar

1 c. white sugar

2 eggs, beaten

1 1/2 c. flour

1 tsp. soda

1 tsp. cinnamon

TOPPING:

6 tbsp. melted butter or margarine

1/2 c. brown sugar

1/2 c. coconut

1/2 c. chopped nuts (optional)

1/2 tsp. vanilla

Pour boiling water over oats; stir and cool. Cream together butter, brown sugar, white sugar, eggs. Sift together flour, soda, cinnamon and add to creamed mixture. Add oats; mix well.

MENNONITE SPICY FUDGE PUDDING

1 c Sifted all-purpose flour
2 tsp Baking powder
3/4 c Sugar
1/8 tsp Salt
2 tbsp Cocoa
3/4 tsp Cinnamon
1/4 tsp Cloves

Combine
1/2 c Milk
1/2 tsp Vanilla
2 tbsp Melted butter

Add to dry ingredients and stir just until smooth.
Spread over bottom of 8 inch square buttered pan.
Combine and sprinkle over batter, 1/2 cup firmly packed brown sugar and 1/2 cup white sugar. Pour 1 cup cold water over entire mixture.

Do not stir. Bake at 325F. for 40 minutes or until top is firm to a light touch.

APPLE DESSERT

5 to 6 med apples
1/4 c butter
2 c brown sugar
1 tsp lemon juice
Grated peel of 1/2 a lemon
2 large egg yolks
1 c sugar
1/2 c cold water
1 tsp vanilla
1 c all-purpose flour
1/2 tsp salt
1 tsp baking powder
2 large egg whites

Pare, core and slice apples. Melt butter in a deep, 9" round cake pan, add brown sugar and stir until well mixed. Top with apples and sprinkle with lemon juice and peel. Beat egg yolks and sugar until light and pale yellow. Mix water and vanilla. Stir flour with salt and baking powder and add to egg mixture alternately with vanilla mixture. Beat egg whites until stiff, fold into batter and pour over apples.

Bake at 350 degree F oven for 45 to 50 minutes. Serve hot or tepid, and it is best not to unmold the pudding.

LEMON PIE

COOK TOGETHER:

1 cup molasses or maple syrup

1 cup brown sugar

2 cups hot water

1 egg, beaten

SECOND PART:

1 cup granulated sugar

1/2 cup lard

1 egg

1 cup sour milk or cream

2 cups flour

1/2 tsp. soda

2 tsp. baking powder

Mix second part like you would mix a cake. Divide batter into four unbaked pie shells. Pour syrup over the batter and bake at 400 for 10 minutes, then reduce heat to 350 and bake until done. Cake will rise to top during baking.

WEDDING ROLLS

3 1/2 cups milk

1 Tbsp. yeast

1 tsp. honey

3 Tbsp. butter

1/4 cup butter

1/2 cup sugar

1/4 cup honey

1 small egg

8 cups flour

Warm the milk to lukewarm. Dissolve yeast with 1 tsp. honey and 1/2 cup milk. Melt the butter and combine with milk, honey, sugar and egg. Mix well. Add flour. Knead and let rise 1 hour. Knead a second time and let rise 2 hours. Form the buns and let rise 1 hour. Bake at 450F for 10–15 minutes. Makes 30 large buns.

ALYMER ONTARIO CINNAMON ROLLS

4 cups milk (scalded)
1 cup margarine
5 eggs
1 1/2 tablespoons salt
1 /2 cup sugar
2 tablespoon yeast dissolved in warm water

Mix everything together. Mix flour into mixture as needed. Keep on sticky side. Let rise till double the size. Roll out on floured surface to 1/2-inch thickness. Spread butter or margarine on then sprinkle with brown sugar and cinnamon. Add raisins if desired. Roll up and cut it into 1-inch pieces. Put on oiled sheet and let rise. Bake till brown.

POPPY SEED BUNS

2 eggs, beaten
1 cup sugar
flour to make a medium paste
1 tbsp. cinnamon
2 cups raisins
1 tbsp. vanilla

Dough:
2 tsp. yeast
1 tsp. sugar
1/2 cup milk, lukewarm

Mix and let rise. Add the following:
1 1/2 cup scalded milk
1/2 cup sugar
2/3 cup margarine
1/2 tsp. salt
4 cups flour

Make into a soft dough. Let rise 1 hour. Roll out thin and cut into squares. Place 1 - 2 Tbsp of filling on each square. Roll up and pinch together. Let rise 30 minutes. Bake at 350F for 30 minutes

AMISH MAPLE CRÈME CAKE

maple syrup
Pinch salt
--TOPPING:--
2 c. whipping cream
1/2 c. powdered sugar
2 tsp. vanilla
Pinch salt

Cook on low heat, very slow, stirring constantly until it bubbles in the middle. Pour into a baked pie shell. Chill for 1 hour. Whip ingredients until thick. Pour on top of pie filling and sprinkle with chopped pecans.

HALF MOONS

2 c. cold water
1/8 tsp. salt
2 c. sugar
1 orange, juice and grated rind
1 tbsp. cinnamon
1 recipe (double crust) pie pastry

Cook the dried apples in a saucepan with water and the salt. When apples are soft and pulpy. Add the sugar, orange and cinnamon. Simmer until water is cooked away. Roll pastry out and cut in 8 inch circles. Place generous portions of the mixture on half of the pastry rounds; fold the pastry over and pinch the edges tightly together. Bake in 450 degree oven for 10 minutes. Reduce heat to 350 degrees and bake about 35 to 40 minutes longer or until golden brown. Makes 6 half moon pies.

RHUBARB MERINGUE PIE

3 c. diced rhubarb
1 1/4 c. sugar
1/4 tsp. salt
2 tbsp. water
1 1/2 Tbsp. cornstarch
3 tbsp. cold water
1 tbsp. lemon juice
4 eggs, separated
1 9" pie shell

Combine rhubarb, 1 c. sugar, salt and 2 Tbsp. water in a saucepan. Bring to boil over low heat. Dissolve cornstarch in 3 Tbsp. cold water and add to rhubarb mix. Cook, stirring constantly, until clear and thick. Add lemon juice and slightly beaten egg yolks. Remove from heat.

Beat 2 egg whites until stiff but not dry. Fold into rhubarb mix. Pour into pie shell. Beat remaining egg whites until soft peaks form. Gradually add remaining 1/4 c. sugar and beat well. Spoon meringue over rhubarb mixture.

Bake at 350 degrees for about 15 minutes or until meringue is lightly brown.

CARROT CAKE

1/4 cup veg. oil

2 teaspoon. soda

3 large eggs

1 tsp. salt

2 cups sugar

2 tsp. cinnamon

2 cups flour

3 cups grated carrots

2 tsp. baking powder

1 cup chopped walnuts [or pecans]

Sift dry ingredients together, mix thoroughly the sugar, oil, and eggs. Add carrots and mix. Add dry ingredients a little at a time. Add nuts. Bake in greased and floured 9 x 13 pan at 325% for 60 to 70 minutes.

Frost with cream cheese frosting

1 8oz. cream cheese

1 stick oleo

1 lb. powdered sugar

1 cup chopped nuts

SOUR CHERRY PIE

1 quart fresh sour cherries, pitted
1 1/2 cups sugar
1/2 cup flour
pie crust

Mix flour, sugar and cherries in a bowl. Fill unbaked pie crust with the cherries. Put on the top crust and poke holes or slits to vent. Bake in a 450 degree oven for 10 minutes, then reduce to 350 degrees for 20-30 minutes.

AMISH PIE

Bottom:
1/2 cup molasses
1/2 cup sugar
1 egg
1 cup water
2 tbs flour
Juice and rind of 1/2 lemon
Top:
2/3 cup sugar
1/4 cup butter

1 egg
1/2 tsp baking soda
1/2 cup sour milk
1 1/4 cup flour

Combine ingredients for bottom of pie. Pour into unbaked pie shell (9 in.) For topping: combine butter and sugar. Add egg and beat thoroughly. Add milk and sifted dry ingredients alternately. Spread topping over mixture in pie shell. Bake at 375 degrees for0 35 or 40 minutes.

MENNONITE APPLE DUMPLINGS

2 cups all-purpose flour
4 teaspoons baking powder
1 teaspoon salt
4 tablespoons shortening
1 cup milk
4 or 5 apples pared, cored and cut in half
Sugar
1 teaspoon cinnamon

Sift the dry ingredients, cut in shortening, add milk and mix to a smooth dough. Turn onto a floured board and divide into 8 or 10 portions; roll out each portion large enough to cover 1/2 apple. Place apple on each piece of dough, fill core hollow with sugar and cinnamon. Wet edges of dough and press together over apple. Place on greased baking sheet and bake at 350 degrees F until the apples are tender - about 1/2 hour. Serve with boiled Brown Sugar Sauce or put the dumplings into a baking dish, pour the uncooked ingredients for Brown Sugar Sauce into the pan around them and bake until the dumplings are done and the sauce is thick.

Brown Sugar Sauce
2 cups water
2 cups brown sugar
3 tablespoons butter
Combine and cook together for 5 minutes; or simply pour uncooked sauce around dumplings and bake.

MENNONITE BREAD PUDDING

2 eggs, well beaten

1/2 cup granulated sugar

2 cups milk

1/4 teaspoon nutmeg, ground

4 cups day old bread (1/2-inch slices), cubed

1/4 cup raisins

Beat eggs. Add sugar, milk and nutmeg. Butter a 1 1/2-quart baking dish. Put bread cubes into dish and pour egg mixture over the bread. Let the bread cubes become soaked by the mixture. Mix in the raisins. Bake at 350 degrees F for 25 minutes. Serve warm.

MENNONITE CARMEL FROSTING

3 cups packed brown suga1r

1 cup top milk or thin cream

2 tablespoons butter

1 teaspoon vanilla extract

Mix ingredients together in a saucepan. Stir until sugar is dissolved; cook syrup until it forms a soft ball when dropped in cold water (238 degrees F). Cool until you can hold your hand on the bottom of the pan. Beat until creamy and spread on cake.

MENNONITE MAPLE WALNUT CAKE

1/3 cup soft butter or regular margarine

2 eggs

1 cup maple syrup

1 1/4 cups all-purpose white flour

2 teaspoons baking powder

Pinch salt

1 cup walnuts, chopped not too fine

Beat together butter, eggs, and syrup. This will look curdled don't worry. Sift together flour, baking powder, and salt, and stir in gradually. Beat with whisk until smooth fold in walnuts.

Pour into a greased square pan and bake at 350 degrees F for about 25 to 30 minutes or until done. Let cool before icing with a maple butter icing.

Maple Butter Icing

Melt 2 tablespoons butter, blend in a cupful of sifted icing sugar and moisten to a spreading consistency with maple syrup.

MENNONITE OATMEAL BREAD

2 cups rolled oats (preferably coarse)

2 cups boiling water

1/2 cup molasses

1/2 cup brown sugar

1 teaspoon salt

1/2 cup shortening

1/2 cup lukewarm water

1 teaspoon sugar

2 packets yeast (about 2 tablespoon)

Chopped nuts (optional)

Raisins (optional)

About 6 cups all-purpose flour

Pour boiling water over rolled oats; stir and add molasses, salt, brown sugar and shortening. Let stand until lukewarm, then add yeast dissolved in warm water with sugar. Mix in flour until it requires muscle. Then knead a few minutes on well floured surface. Put dough in bowl; cover. Let rise 1 to 2 hours in warm, draft-free place to double its size (rolls and buns take less time to rise and bake; can make various shapes). It is risen enough if the dent stays when you press your fingers deeply into it. Nuts or raisins may be added with flour or kneaded into individual loaves. Divide into 2 loaves; let rise again until smooth and round over tops of pans, about an hour or more. Bake at 400 degrees F for 35 minutes.

Rye Bread variation
Use half rye and half all-purpose flour and use 1/2 cup molasses as part of the liquid.

APPLESAUCE CAKE

1/2 cup butter

1 cup granulated or brown sugar

1 cup applesauce

1 cup all-purpose flour

1/2 teaspoon salt

1/2 teaspoon baking powder

1 teaspoon baking soda

1/2 teaspoon cloves

1 teaspoon cinnamon

1 teaspoon allspice

1 cup raisins

1/4 cup chopped nuts

Cream butter; add sugar, beat until light. Add egg; beat until fluffy. Add applesauce; mix well.

Sift together flour, salt, baking powder, soda, cloves, cinnamon and allspice. Add nuts and raisins. Combine two mixtures. Bake in a greased 8-inch square pan at 350 degrees F for 40 to 45 minutes.

Frost with vanilla or chocolate frosting, if desired.

BANANA CAKE

1/2 cup butter

2 cups all-purpose flour, sifted

1 cup sour milk

1 teaspoon vanilla extract

1 1/2 cups granulated sugar

1 teaspoon baking powder

1 teaspoon baking soda

2 bananas, creamed

2 eggs, beaten

Cream butter and sugar together. Add well beaten eggs. To this mixture, add the sour milk alternately with the sifted flour, baking powder and the baking soda. Add creamed bananas and vanilla extract. Beat with an egg beater. Grease and flour a pan and bake cake at 350 degrees F for about 40 minutes. Cool before removing from pan

GREEN TOMATO BREAD

3 eggs

1-1/2 cups sugar

1 cup vegetable oil

1 teaspoon salt

1 tablespoon vanilla

2 cups grated, drained, green tomatoes

3 cups flour

1-1/4 teaspoons baking soda

1/2 teaspoon baking powder

3/4 cup raisins

1 cup chopped nuts

Beat eggs well. Add sugar, oil, salt, vanilla, and tomatoes.

Sift dry ingredients together. Gradually add to tomato mixture. Stir in raisins and nuts.

Pour into greased bread pans and bake at 350 degrees for 45 minutes.

Makes 2 loaves

HOMEMADE WALNUT BREAD

3 cups sifted flour

1 cup sugar

4 teaspoons baking powder

1-1/2 teaspoons salt

1 egg, lightly beaten

1/4 cup shortening, melted

1-1/2 cups milk

1 teaspoon vanilla

1-1/2 cups walnuts, coarsely chopped

Sift together flour, sugar, baking powder, and salt.

Combine egg, shortening, milk, and vanilla and add to dry mixture. Stir just until all flour is moistened. Stir in walnuts.

Turn into a greased loaf pan or divide between two greased 2-1/2 pound cans. Bake at 350 degrees for 80 minutes for loaf pan or about 70 minutes for cans.

MENNONITE RHUBARB CRUNCH

2 cups flour
1-1/2 cups uncooked oatmeal
2 cups brown sugar
1 cup butter, melted
2 teaspoons cinnamon
8 cups fresh rhubarb, diced
2 cups sugar
4 tablespoons cornstarch
2 cups water
2 teaspoons vanilla

Combine flour, oatmeal, brown sugar, melted butter and cinnamon together until crumbly.

Press half of the crumb mixture into a greased 9 x 2 x 13-inch cake pan; set remaining crumb mixture aside to use as topping.

Combine sugar, cornstarch, water and vanilla in a saucepan. Cook on medium-high heat until thick and clear, about 10 to 12 minutes, stirring constantly.

Place diced rhubarb on top of crumb mixture in cake pan. Pour cooked mixture over top of rhubarb; then top with remaining crumb mixture.

Bake at 350 degrees for 1 hour.

MENNONITE BROCCOLI BREAD

2 (1-pound) loaves frozen bread dough, thawed
1 or 2 heads fresh broccoli, cut into florets with no stems
1 can pitted black olives, chopped
Garlic powder
Olive oil
Red pepper flakes
Grated cheese
Salt and pepper, to taste

Cook broccoli florets, no stems, until tender. Drain, let cool, squeeze out any excess liquid, and chop fine.
Flatten out thawed bread loaves into individual long rectangles on a lightly floured surface.
Sprinkle cooled, chopped broccoli on top of flattened bread. Sprinkle chopped black olives and red pepper flakes over broccoli. Salt and pepper, to taste.

Drizzle olive oil sparingly over vegetables, then sprinkle with grated cheese to cover thinly. Sprinkle with garlic powder on top of cheese.
Roll up lengthwise; tuck ends under and pinch short ends closed. Bake on parchment paper covered

cookie sheet at 350 degrees until golden brown. Remove and place on wire racks to cool.

Cut into slices and serve with a salad or as an appetizer to your meal.

AMISH PUDDING

1 cup granulated sugar

1 egg

1 teaspoon baking powder

1/2 cup milk

1 teaspoon vanilla extract

Butter, the size of a walnut

Flour, as needed

Chocolate Pudding Filling

1 1/2 cups milk

1 1/2 cups water

1/2 cup granulated sugar

2 tablespoons cornstarch

1 tablespoon all-purpose flour

2 tablespoons cocoa powder

1 teaspoon vanilla extract

Cream the butter and egg; add the sugar and baking powder; mix well; add the milk and vanilla extract; mix well. Add enough flour to make a little stiffer than cake batter and bake in 9x13-inch pan at 375 degrees F for 20-30 minutes. When cool cut in little squares and top with filling.

Chocolate Pudding Filling: Mix sugar, flour, cornstarch and cocoa, add to milk and water and bring to boil, add vanilla. Put this on the squares and serve while hot

AMISH CRUMB TOP PEACH PIE

6 sliced peaches
1 unbaked pie shell
1/4 cup all-purpose flour
3/4 cup granulated sugar
1 cup cream
1/3 cup all-purpose flour
1/3 cup granulated sugar
3 tablespoons butter

Arrange peaches in shell. Mix flour, 3/4 cup sugar, cream and pour over peaches. Mix flour, 1/3 cup sugar and butter and put on top of pie. Bake at 425 degrees F for 10 minutes, then at 350 degrees F until custard is set - about 30 minutes.

HOT CHOCOLATE TAPIOCA

1 tablespoon cocoa

1/2 cup granulated sugar

Add 2 cups boiling water

1 teaspoon vanilla extract

1/2 teaspoon salt

1 cup tapioca

1/2 cup brown sugar

Add more water until right consistency.

Serve hot with cold milk.

JAM CAKE

2 cups granulated sugar

4 cups all-purpose flour

1/2 cup butter or more

2 cups blackberry jam

1 cup black walnuts (or nuts of choice)

1 cup raisins or more

2 teaspoons cinnamon

2 teaspoons cloves

2 teaspoons nutmeg

2 teaspoons allspice

2 teaspoons baking soda, dissolved in 1 cup buttermilk

6 eggs or more

Place all ingredients in a large pan and mix thoroughly. Bake in a 13 x 9-inch baking pan at 300 F degrees for about an hour. Pour icing over cake while cake is hot.

Icing

2 cups granulated sugar

1 cup sweet milk

1/2 cup butter

Cook until about as thick as cream. Have icing cooked and ready to put on cake as soon as cake is done. Pour on while icing and cake are both hot.

MAPLE CREAM PIE

Filling

1 can sweetened condensed milk

2/3 cup maple syrup

Pinch salt

Topping

2 cups whipping cream

1/2 cup powdered sugar

2 teaspoons vanilla extract

Pinch salt

Chopped pecans

Filling: Cook sweetened condensed milk, maple syrup and salt over low heat, stirring constantly until it bubbles in the middle. Pour into a baked pie shell. Chill for 1 hour.

Topping: Whip whipping cream, powdered sugar, vanilla extract and salt until thick. Pour on top of pie filling and sprinkle with chopped pecans.

MILK PIE

3 eggs

1 cup molasses

1 cup granulated sugar

1/2 cup flour

1 teaspoon baking soda

3 cups thick sour milk

2 (9-inch) unbaked pie shells

Preheat oven to 400 degrees F.

Beat eggs. Add molasses. Combine sugar, flour and baking soda and add to egg mixture. Add thick milk. Pour into unbaked pie shells. Bake for 10 minutes; then reduce oven temperature to 325 degrees F and bake for 40 to 45 minutes. Sprinkle top of pie with cinnamon, if desired.

BROWN SUGAR ANGEL FOOD CAKE

2 cups (14 to 16) egg whites

1 1/2 teaspoons cream of tartar

2 teaspoons vanilla extract

1 teaspoon salt

2 cups brown sugar, firmly packed

1 1/2 cups sifted cake flour

Beat the egg whites with the cream of tartar, vanilla and salt until stiff peaks form. Gradually sift 1 cup of the sugar into the beaten whites and beat to incorporate.

Sift remaining sugar with all the flour and gently fold it into the whites. Gently turn the batter into an ungreased 10-inch tube pan and bake at 350 degrees F for 45 to 50 minutes. (When done, the cake should spring back at the touch of a finger.) Let cake cool before serving.

CHEESE PIE

Filling

3 eggs

1/2 teaspoon lemon extract

16 ounces cream cheese

Pinch of salt

Topping

6 tablespoons granulated sugar

1 teaspoon vanilla extract

2 cups sour cream

Have cream cheese at room temperature. Put all filling ingredients in mixer bowl; beat thoroughly. Bake in a pie plate very lightly greased with vegetable oil for 30 minutes at 325 degrees F (350 degrees F if using tin or aluminum). Cool 20 minutes.

Topping: Mix ingredients and pour over top and return to oven and bake 10 minutes. Cool. Refrigerate.

QUICK SOURDOUGH

Yield: 4 loaves (64 slices)

2 3/4 cups warm skim milk

1/4 cup low fat buttermilk

4 3/4 cups all-purpose flour

1/4 cup whole wheat flour

3 cups plus 1 teaspoon granulated sugar

1 package active dry yeast

2/3 cup canola oil

1 1/4 teaspoons baking powder

1 egg

1 teaspoon ground cinnamon

1 teaspoon vanilla extract

1/2 teaspoon baking soda

2 cups very coarsely chopped hazelnuts

2 cups dried cherries

Preheat oven to 350 degrees F.

In a large nonreactive bowl, mix 3/4 cup of the skim milk, the buttermilk, 3/4 cup of the all purpose flour, the whole wheat flour, 1 teaspoon sugar, and the yeast. Set aside for 10 minutes or until the mixture starts to bubble.

In a large mixing bowl, place the remaining ingredients, mix 2 cups skim milk, 4 cups flour, 3 cups sugar, oil, baking powder, egg, cinnamon, vanilla, salt, baking soda, except for the hazelnuts and cherries, and mix well. Add the milk yeast mixture to the bowl and mix well. Fold in the hazelnuts and cherries.

Lightly grease four 10 x 5 x 2-inch pans with vegetable oil, divide the dough among the pans, and bake for 1 hour and 10 minutes, or until a wooden pick inserted in the center comes out clean.

SALT RISING BREAD

2 1/2 cups potatoes, sliced
2 tablespoons cornmeal
1 1/2 tablespoons salt
1 quart boiling water
1 1/2 teaspoons granulated sugar
1 teaspoon baking soda
1 cup warm milk
1 tablespoon shortening, melted
11 cups flour

Sprinkle 1 tablespoon salt and the cornmeal over potatoes. Add boiling water and stir until salt has dissolved. Cover and keep warm from noon to the following morning.

Drain off liquid into a large bowl. Add the baking soda, 1 1/2 teaspoons sugar and 5 cups flour to the liquid. Stir until ingredients are well blended. This sponge should be the consistency of cake batter. Set mixture in a warm place, and let rise until light and full of bubbles. This requires about 1 1/2 hours.

Scald milk and cool to lukewarm. Add shortening. Add milk and remaining flour to sponge. Knead for 10 to 12 minutes and shape into loaves. Makes 3 medium-size loaves. Let rise until light - about 1 1/2 hours. Bake at 350 degrees F for 1 hour.

SPONGE PUDDING

5 to 6 med apples
1/4 c butter
2 c brown sugar
1 tsp lemon juice
Grated peel of 1/2 a lemon
2 large egg yolks

1 c sugar

1/2 c cold water

1 tsp vanilla

1 c all-purpose flour

1/2 tsp salt

1 tsp baking powder

2 large egg whites

Pare, core and slice apples. Melt butter in a deep, 9" round cake pan, add brown sugar and stir until well mixed. Top with apples and sprinkle with lemon juice and peel. Beat egg yolks and sugar until light and pale yellow. Mix water and vanilla. Stir flour with salt and baking powder and add to egg mixture alternately with vanilla mixture. Beat egg whites until stiff, fold into batter and pour over apples. Bake at 350 degree F oven for 45 to 50 minutes. Serve hot or tepid, and it is best not to unmold the pudding.

SPICY FUDGE PUDDING

1 c Sifted all-purpose flour
2 teaspoons baking powder
3/4 c Sugar
1/8 tsp Salt
2 tbsp Cocoa
3/4 tsp Cinnamon
1/4 tsp Cloves

Combine
1/2 c Milk
1/2 tsp Vanilla
2 tbsp Melted butter

Add to dry ingredients and stir just until smooth. Spread over bottom of 8 inch square buttered pan. Combine and sprinkle over batter, 1/2 cup firmly packed brown sugar and 1/2 cup white sugar. Pour 1 cup cold water over entire mixture. Do not stir. Bake at 325F. for 40 minutes or until top is firm to a light touch.

OATMEAL CAKE

1 c. quick rolled oats
1 1/2 c. boiling water
1/2 c. butter or margarine
1 c. brown sugar
1 c. white sugar
2 eggs, beaten
1 1/2 c. flour
1 tsp. soda
1 tsp. cinnamon

TOPPING:
6 tbsp. melted butter or margarine
1/2 c. brown sugar
1/2 c. coconut
1/2 c. chopped nuts (optional)
1/2 tsp. vanilla

Pour boiling water over oats; stir and cool. Cream together butter, brown sugar, white sugar, eggs. Sift together flour, soda, cinnamon and add to creamed mixture. Add oats; mix well.

COOKIES, CANDIES, & BARS

THE AMISH COOK'S OATMEAL WHOOPIE PIES

Makes: 24 whoopie pies

Ingredients
For the cookies:
3/4 cup (1 1/2 sticks) butter, softened

2 cups packed brown sugar

2 large eggs

1/2 teaspoon salt

2 cups all-purpose flour

1 teaspoon baking powder

1 teaspoon ground cinnamon

2 cups quick-cooking rolled oats

2 teaspoons baking soda

3 tablespoons boiling water

For the filling:
1 large egg white

1 tablespoon vanilla extract

2 tablespoons milk

2 cups powdered sugar

1/4 cups shortening, softened

Directions

Preheat the oven to 425°F. Lightly grease a baking sheet and set aside.

To make the cookies: Cream the butter, sugar, and eggs in a large bowl. In a separate bowl, sift together the salt, flour, and baking powder. Add to the creamed mixture. Add the cinnamon and oats. Mix well. In a small dish, add the baking soda to the boiling water, and then stir the mixture into the rest of the batter. Mix well. Drop by the tablespoon onto the baking sheets about 2 inches apart and bake until the cookies are firm and just starting to turn golden around the edges, 10 to 15 minutes. Cool the cookies on a wire rack or a plate.

To make the filling: Combine the egg white, vanilla, milk, and 1 cup of the powdered sugar. Cream well. Add the remaining 1 cup of sugar and the shortening and beat until smooth. Spread 1 tablespoon of filling (more if desired) on one cookie, and then top with a second cookie.

Wrap each whoopie pie cookie in plastic wrap and then put into sealed containers. These cookies will stay fresh for up to 5 days.

PEANUT BUTTER FUDGE

Editor's Note: This simple fudge recipe was submitted by Mrs. Noah Hostetler in the Amish settlement of Ethridge, Tennessee.

2 cups sugar
1 1/3 cups peanut butter
1/2 cup milk
1 jar (7 ounces) marshmallow crème

In a saucepan bring sugar and milk to a boil. Boil for 3 minutes. Remove from heat. Add peanut butter and marshmallow crème. Mix well. Quickly pour into a buttered 8 inch square pan. Chill until set. Cut into squares.

CAN'T LEAVE ALONE BARS

1 box yellow cake mix
1/3 cup vegetable oil
2 eggs
1 can condensed milk
1 stick butter
1 cup chocolate chips

Melt chocolate chips, butter, and mix in condensed milk. In a cake pan place thin layer of cake batter. Then pour milk mixture over it and top with remaining cake batter.

COCONUT OATMEAL COOKIES

1/2 cup melted butter

1 teaspoon soda

2 eggs, well-beaten

2 cups brown sugar

2 cups flour

4 cups rolled oats

1 cup shredded coconut

1/2 teaspoon vanilla

1/2 cup melted lard

Mix all ingredients, ten roll in waxed paper. Let stand till cool or overnight. Slice and bake at 350.

LIGHT AS A FEATHER DOUGHNUTS

Mrs. Emma Raber in Stevens, Pennsylvania submitted this delicious doughnut recipe!

1 1/2 cups milk, scalded

1/2 cup sugar

1 teaspoon salt

1/2 cup margarine

1 1/2 cup warm water

1/2 tablespoon sugar

2 packages of yeast

2 eggs

8 - 10 cups bread flour

Add sugar, salt, and margarine to hot milk. Cool to lukewarm. Add yeast and sugar to warm water. Let rise for 5 minutes. Pour both liquids together plus eggs and add flour. After last flour has been added knead for 10 minutes. Let rise 1 hour and knead again. Let rise 1 hour and punch down and roll to 1/2 inch and cut. Put on floured pan, let rise and deep fat fry at 350. Glaze while still warm

GLAZE
8 cups powdered sugar
pinch salt
1 teaspoon vanilla
Enough warm water for a medium thickness

YEAST DOUGHNUTS

Editor's Note: This recipe comes from the Martin family in Aylmer, Ontario.

2 1/3 cups lukewarm water
1 package yeast (2 tablespoons even)
Cream together
3 eggs
1/2 cup cream
3/4 cup sugar
1/3 cup oleo or butter

Also add 1 teaspoon vinegar. This is to keep lard from soaking in while frying. Add 6 or 7 cups of flour to make a firm dough. Let rise once then roll out and cut. Let rise again and bake. Put lard over to melt when you start cutting. When hot, bake doughnuts. Doughnuts should rise double before baking. Glaze doughnuts with powdered sugar glaze.

RAISIN-FILLED COOKIES

Editor's Note: This recipe comes to us from an Old Order German Baptist Brethren woman in Indiana. The Old Order German Baptists are a horse-and-buggy very conservative group within the Brethren church, a distinctly separate faith from the Anabaptist Amish.

Dough:

2 cups sugar

1 cup shortening (lard or butter)

2 eggs

1 teaspoon real vanilla

1 cup milk

2 teaspoons baking powder

1 teaspoon baking soda

Flour (enough to roll out a soft dough and cut, about

6 cups)

Filling:

2 cups ground raisins

2 cups water

1 cup sugar

2 tablespoons flour

1 or 1 1/2 cup chopped walnuts

Roll dough out very thin. Using a 3 inch wide biscuit or doughnut cutter, cut enough to fill a cookie sheet.

Put a tablespoons full or a nice big blob of raisin filling in the center of each cookie. Now using the same cutter, cut tops for each cookie. Using a thimble, cut a whole in the center of each of the "top" cookies. Place a top cookie on each of the raisin blobs, sealing all around with fingertip. Bake until done, usually not being brown at all. Grandma usually put them on a newspaper to cool, so I do too!)

MONSTER COOKIES

1 1/2 stick oleo
1 cup white sugar
1 cup brown sugar
4 eggs
1 pound creamy peanut butter cookies
2 1/2 teaspoons baking soda
4 cups oatmeal
1/2 pound M&Ms
12 ounces chocolate chips

Cream sugars and oleo. Add eggs, then add rest of ingredients. Add more oatmeal if necessary to make a stiff dough. Form into teaspoon-size balls and roll in powdered sugar. Bake at 350 for 10 minutes. Do not overbake!

COFFEE COOKIES

1 1/2 cup brown sugar
2 eggs
1 teaspoon vanilla
3/4 teaspoon baking soda
3 cups flour
3/4 cup lard
3/4 cups coffee
1/2 teaspoon salt
2 1/4 teaspoon baking powder

Bake at 350 for 10 minutes. Spread with caramel frosting.

Caramel Frosting:
1 1/2 tablespoons milk
1/2 cup brown sugar
1 teaspoon vanilla
2 1/2 tablespoons butter
Powdered sugar

Cook together for 1 minute then add powdered sugar till easily spread. Frost while frosting is warm.

MAPLE SANDWICH COOKIES

2 cups white sugar

2 cups brown sugar

1 cup margarine, melted

2 eggs

1 1/2 teaspoon baking soda

1 teaspoon baking powder

1 cup milk

1/4 cup (or more) maple flavoring

Pinch of salt

Vanilla flavoring

8 1/2 cups flour

Cream together the sugars and margarine. Add eggs and mix well. Add baking soda, baking powder, salt, and maple flavoring. Mix well. Alternately add the milk and flour. Shape into balls. Roll in white sugar and place on ungreased cookie sheet. Flatten cookie with a drinking glass. Bake at 350 for 12 minutes. Makes around 5 dozen sandwich cookies.

ICING:

5 tablespoons oleo
1 1/2 cups brown sugar
6 tablespoons milk
Pinch of salt
Powdered sugar

Heat oleo and brown sugar to boiling. Remove from heat and let cool. Add milk, salt and powdered sugar to desired consistency.

You may use your own favorite icing. This is a soft, chewy cookie that is good without the icing, too.

AMISH APPLE BROWNIES

1 c butter, softened
1 3/4 c Sugar
2 Eggs, well beaten
1 tsp Vanilla
2 c All-purpose flour
1 tsp Baking powder
1 tsp Baking soda
1 tsp Cinnamon
1/2 tsp Salt
2 c Baking apples, peeled, chopped
1/2 c Pecans or walnuts

In a large mixing bowl, cream butter, sugar, eggs and vanilla. Combine dry ingredients and add to butter mixture.

Mix until flour is moistened. Fold in apples and nuts. Spread in a greased 9 x 9 inch baking pan and bake in 350 degree oven 45 minutes or until done.

EASY AMISH SUGAR COOKIES

Cream together:
2 sticks butter
1 cup sugar
1 cup brown sugar
2 large eggs
1/2 tsp salt
1 tsp vanilla

Set aside: 1 cup milk

Mix together:
5 1/2 cups flour
2 tsp baking soda
1 tsp baking soda
generous dash of nutmeg, cinnamon, allspice

Mix 1/2 dry & 1/2 creamed with 1/2 c milk. Add 1/2 dry to mix, 1/2 creamed, and last 1/2c milk.

Dough should be stiff. If needed, add more flour to stiffen. Chill at least 1 hour. Roll out dough on floured board to desired thickness, and cut out with cookie cutters.

AMISH PRETZEL PUDDING

In a bowl mix

2 c crushed pretzels

1/2 c melted butter

3 tbsp sugar

In separate bowl mix

8 oz cream cheese (softened)

2 c powdered sugar

once the sugar and cheese are mixed, add

2 c small marshmallows

1 c whipped cream

In 2 1/4 c boiling water, mix

6 oz strawberry jello

10 oz sliced strawberries.

Add to crushed pretzel mix
fold in cream cheese mix
Put in buttered or greased casserole baking dish
Bake 375 for 40-45 mins til done.

Serve warm with ice cream and whipped cream.

CHOCOLATE CHIP COOKIES

1/2 c. shortening
1 c. sugar
2 lg. eggs
1/2 c. milk
2 1/2 c. flour
1 tsp. baking powder
3/4 tsp. baking soda (place in the milk)
1 (12 oz.) bag chocolate chips or butterscotch chips

Cream shortening and sugar. Add eggs and milk with soda. Mix together and add baking powder. Gradually add flour and stir well. Stir in chocolate chips or butterscotch chips. Place on a greased cookie sheet about 1teaspoon of dough. Bake at 400 degrees until the edge is lightly brown.

AMISH HATS

2 cups margarine
4 eggs
2 teaspoons baking soda
2 teaspoons salt
4 cups granulated sugar
7 cups all-purpose flour
3/4 cups cocoa powder
2 teaspoons vanilla extract
Large marshmallows, cut in half
Chocolate frosting

Mix margarine, eggs, baking soda, salt, sugar, flour and cocoa powder and drop by teaspoon onto a cookie sheet. Bake 8 minutes at 375 degrees F. Remove from oven and put half a marshmallow on top of each cookie. Bake in oven only until marshmallow is slightly puffed. Put chocolate frosting on top when cooled.

AMISH WHOOPIE PIES

2 cups sugar

1 cup shortening

2 eggs

4 cups flour

1 cup baking cocoa

2 tsp. vanilla

1 tsp. salt

1 cup sour milk

2 tsp. baking soda

1 cup hot water

Directions:

1. Cream sugar and shortening. Add eggs.
2. Sift together flour, cocoa, and salt.
3. Add to creamed mixture alternately with sour milk.
4. Add the vanilla and dissolve soda in hot water and add last. Mix well.

LARGE BATCH AMISH FUDGE

1 pound margarine
1 pound Velveeta cheese
2 cups nuts, chopped (if desired)
1 cup cocoa powder
2 tablespoons vanilla extract
4 pounds confectioners' sugar

Melt together margarine and cheese. Add nuts, cocoa and vanilla extract; slowly add confectioners' sugar in small amounts; beat well. Pour into buttered pans; chill. Cut into squares.

OATMEAL CINNAMON CRISPIES

2 1/2 cups butter, softened
5 cups granulated sugar
1/3 cup dark molasses
4 eggs
4 teaspoons baking powder
1 teaspoon baking soda
2 teaspoons salt
1 tablespoon cinnamon
1 tablespoon vanilla extract

4 1/3 cups flour
4 1/3 cups old fashioned oats
2 cups finely chopped pecans

Preheat oven 375 degrees F. Grease 2 cookie sheets. Cream first 3 ingredients. Beat in eggs one at a time. Add baking powder, baking soda, salt, cinnamon and vanilla extract. Beat until well blended. Add flour and blend. Add oats and nuts and blend. Drop by rounded spoonful onto prepared cookie sheets. Bake for 5 to 9 minutes. It may be necessary to turn sheets around so they brown evenly. Let cool on sheets for about 3 minutes. Remove to wire rack till cool. Cookies will look medium brown and crinkly. These freeze well.

SNACKS, APPETIZERS, & DRINKS

QUICK CARAMEL CORN

1 cup brown sugar
1 stick oleo
8 large marshmallows
6 quarts popped corn

Melt sugar, oleo, and marshmallows together. Pour over popcorn and stir well. Enjoy!

CREAMY CARAMEL DIP

8 ounces of cream cheese
3/4 cup brown sugar
1 cup sour cream
2 teaspoons vanilla
2 teaspoons Real Lemon
1 cup milk
3 ounces instant vanilla pudding

Beat cream cheese and sugar until smooth. Add sour cream, vanilla, and Real Lemon. Beat again. Add pudding and milk, beating very well. Serve with fresh fruit. Delicious!

HOMEMADE EGG NOG

5 cups milk
5 eggs
1/2 cup sugar
1 teaspoons vanilla
1/8 teaspoon nutmeg
1/8 teaspoon salt
Handful of ice cubs

Combine everything in blender until ice is shredded. Serve cold.

HOT CHOCOLATE MIX

Editor's Note: This recipe comes to us from an Amish woman in Michigan and who could argue that on a cold winter day in Michigan this delicious hot chocolate or cappachino is a good warmer!

1 box dry milk
8 ounces coffee creamer
1 teaspoon salt
2 boxes instant vanilla pudding
1/2 cup cocoa
1 pound instant chocolate mix (Nestle Quick)

2 cups powdered sugar
Optional: small marshmallows
Cappachinio mix: 3/4 cup instead coffee instead of
Nestle Quik Chocolate

WHITE TRASH

Editor's Note: This recipe with the startling title comes to us from the Amish settlement outside of Vanceburg, Kentucky.

6 cups corn chex
1 pound M & Ms
4 cups pretzel sticks, broken
2 cups salted pretzels
1 1/4 cup white chocolate melted

Mix dry ingredients together. Pour melted chocolate over the dry mix. Toss to coat. Spread onto greased cookie sheets. Cool. Break into pieces.

RHUBARB DRINK

6 gallons of juice (use 1 quart water for each pound of
rhubarb to make juice)
2 cans frozen orange juice
3 46-ounce cans pineapple juice
Sugar to taste - approximately 1 bag (5 pounds)
2 tropical punch envelopes of Kool-Aid

This makes two 20 quart stock pots full. It can be put
into jars and cold packed for 5 minutes or put into
containers and frozen. Add 7Up to partially thawed
drink for a slushy cold treat.

AMISH CARAMEL CORN

7 quarts plain popped popcorn
2 cups dry roasted peanuts (optional)
2 cups brown sugar
1/2 cup light corn syrup
1 teaspoon salt
1 cup margarine
1/2 teaspoon baking soda
1 teaspoon vanilla extract

Place the popped popcorn into two shallow greased baking pans. You may use roasting pans, jelly roll pans, or disposable roasting pans. Add the peanuts to the popped corn if using. Set aside.

Preheat the oven to 250 degrees F (120 degrees C). Combine the brown sugar, corn syrup, margarine and salt in a saucepan. Bring to a boil over medium heat, stirring enough to blend. Once the mixture begins to boil, boil for 5 minutes while stirring constantly.

Remove from the heat, and stir in the baking soda and vanilla. The mixture will be light and foamy. Immediately pour over the popcorn in the pans, and stir to coat. Don't worry too much at this point about getting all of the corn coated.

Bake for 1 hour, removing the pans, and giving them each a good stir every 15 minutes. Line the counter top with waxed paper. Dump the corn out onto the waxed paper and separate the pieces. Allow to cool completely, then store in airtight containers or resealable bags.

AMISH CRACKER JACK

3 qt. popped corn
1 c. brown sugar
1/2 c. butter
1/4 c. corn syrup
1/2 tsp. salt
1/8 tsp. cream of tartar

Cook all except popped corn over medium heat to 260 degree or hard ball. Boil slowly. Pour over popped corn. Put in 200 degree oven for 1 hour. Stir 3 times during the hour. Let cool.

MENNONITE LEMONADE

6 lemons
1 cup granulated sugar
1 quart ice water
A tray of ice cubes
Mint for garnish (optional)

Wash the lemons; cut them into 1/4-inch slices Put the slices in a stainless steel or other non-reactive bowl and add the sugar. Using a wooden spoon or a potato masher, grind down on the lemon slices to release the juice. Let the slices sit for 20 minutes or so, until a syrup forms. Stir now and again. In several bunches, squeeze the lemon slices hard with your hands to extract all the juice, discarding the lemon slices as you go. Strain the juice through a sieve and discard the seeds. Mix the quart of ice water with the lemon juice, adding a little more water if you want a milder-tasting lemonade. Transfer to a pitcher. Chill in the refrigerator or add a tray of ice cubes and serve right away. Garnish each glass with a sprig of mint, if desired.

MISCELLANEOUS RECIPES, ETC.

RED BEET JELLY

3 cups red beet juice
4 cups sugar
1 package sure-gel mixed with 1-6 ounce package
raspberry or Cherry Jello

Bring juice to a boil quickly. Add jello and sure-jell.
Take from heat and add sugar.

CHILDREN'S GUNK

First bowl: mix together 2 cups Elmer's glue and 1 1/2 cup water.
Second bowl: dissolve 2 level teaspoons of 20 Mule Team Borax in 1 cup water. Slowly ad and stir this to glue mixture. Use hands to mix thoroughly. Add any food coloring. Store in refrigertor in ziplock bag or glass jar. Children love to play with this.

WHY USE RECIPES?

The soup was too hot
I guessed the water
It dried in the pot
I guess the salt
And what do you think?
We did nothing all day
But drink!
I guessed the sugar
The sauce as too sweet
And so by guessing
I spoiled our treat
So now I guess nothing,
For cooking by guess
Is sure to result
In a terrible mess.

THE APRON

One day I went to Grandma's
And she was wearing something funny
When I asked her what it was she said
"Why it's a cooking apron, honey."

You wear it when you're cooking
So you don't mess up your clothes
When I asked if I could have too
She replied "Well, I suppose."

So the next time I went to Grandma's
She had a little surprise
She told me to turn around
And to close my little eyes

She had sewn me a little white apron
With hearts of yellow, red and blue
And as she put it on me, she whispered
"Now you can d some cooking, too."

I loved that little apron
And it wore it all the day
When we made some special cookies
And even after when we went to play

I wanted to take it home with me
But Grandma said "no" it should stay
So I left it in the drawer by hers
For our next big cooking day

MINCEMEAT

Editor's Note: This recipe comes to us from the Vanceburg, Kentucky Amish settlement. The Vanceburg community started in May of 2005. 18 families live there as of this printing.

1 1/2 gallons apples
2 tin cups raisins
4 tin cups sugar
2 tin cups beef
4 tin cups cider
2 tablespoons cloves
1 tablespoon allspice

Put in jars and cold pack 1 hour.

ZUCCHINI RELISH

10 cups shredded zucchini
1 teaspoon celery seed
4 cups chopped onion
3 tablespoons cornstarch
5 tablespoons canning salt
4 1/2 cups sugar
1 tablespoon tumeric

2 large peppers
1 tablespoon dry mustard
1 teaspoon mustard seed

Mix first 3 ingredients in large bowl and let set overnight. Rinse the next day and drain well. Add remaining ingredients to zucchini and cook for 30 minutes over low heat. Process 15 minutes in hot water bath. You may put mustard seed and celery seed in a cloth bag to take out when done cooking. For a good tartar sauce mix equal amounts of mayonnaise and relish.

HOMEMADE AMISH OATMEAL

1-1/2 cups quick cooking oats
1/2 cup sugar
1/2 cup milk
1/4 cup butter, melted
1 egg
1 teaspoon baking powder
3/4 teaspoon salt
1 teaspoon vanilla extract
Warm milk
Fresh fruit and/or brown sugar, optional

Combine the first eight ingredients; mix well. Spread evenly in a greased 13-in. x 9-in. baking pan. Bake at 350° for 25–30 minutes or until edges are golden brown. Immediately spoon into bowls; add milk. Top with fruit and/or brown sugar if desired. **Yield:** 6 servings

AMISH NOODLES

3 eggs
2 c. flour (approximately)
1/2 tsp. salt

Beat 3 eggs until frothy, add and stir flour until dough texture. Knead until smooth. Turn into floured cutting board. Roll dough turning often until thin, let noodle dough dry 45 minutes - turn and dry 1/2 hour. Cut into noodles size. Drop into boiling beef or chicken stock, reduce heat and cook at rolling boil about 20 minutes. Noodles boiling, begin their own gravy - season to taste.

MENNONITE WHOLE STRAWBERRY JAM

1 qt. fresh strawberries
1 qt. sugar
1 tbsp. cold water

Wash and drain fruit for a short time. Place berries and sugar in a large kettle. Add cold water. Place over very slow heat until the sugar is melted. Turn heat up higher and when fruit begins to boil, check the clock and boil well for exactly 10 minutes. Remove from heat. Skim and pour into shallow platters where fruit will not be more than 1 inch deep. Leave overnight. In the morning, each berry will be lying in a delicious thick syrup. Bottle in cold, sterilized jars. Yield: 2 quarts.

Made in the USA
Columbia, SC
23 August 2017